KT-117-732

CONTENTS

Chapter 1 Globalisation

Chapter 2 Global Trade

OTHER TITLES IN THE ISSUES SERIES

For more on these titles, visit: www.independence.co.uk

A note on critical evaluation

Because the information reprinted here is from a number of different sources, readers should bear in mind the origin of the text and whether the source is likely to have a particular bias when presenting information (just as they would if undertaking their own research). It is hoped that, as you read about the many aspects of the issues explored in this book, you will critically evaluate the information presented. It is important that you decide whether you are being presented with facts or opinions. Does the writer give a biased or an unbiased report? If an opinion is being expressed, do you agree with the writer?

Globalisation and Trade offers a useful starting point for those who need convenient access to information about the many issues involved. However, it is only a starting point. Following each article is a URL to the relevant organisation's website, which you may wish to visit for further information.

Globalisation and Trade

Volume 226

Series Editor

Lisa Firth

Independence

Educational Publishers

Cambridge

First published by Independence

The Studio, High Green

Great Shelford

Cambridge CB22 5EG

England

© Independence 2012

British Library Cataloguing in Publication Data

Globalisation and trade. -- (Issues ; v. 226)

1. Globalization--Social aspects. 2. Globalization--

Economic aspects.

I. Series II. Firth, Lisa.

303.4'82-dc23

ISBN-13: 978 1 86168 615 2

Printed in Great Britain

MWL Print Group Ltd

Globalisation: key issues

Information from the Trades Union Congress (TUC).

Globalisation defined...

Globalisation is a term that is frequently used but seldom defined. It refers to the rapid increase in the share of economic activity taking place across national boundaries.

This goes beyond the international trade in goods and includes the way those goods are produced, the delivery and sale of services, and the movement of capital.

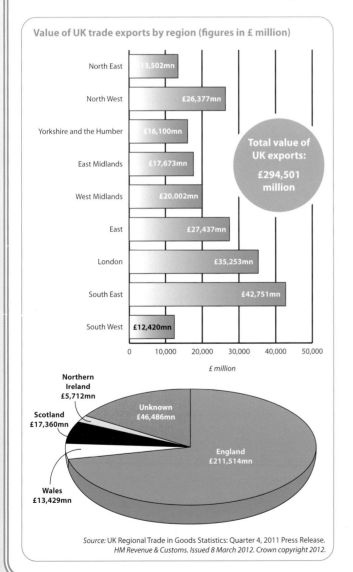

Value of UK trade exports by region (figures in £ million)

North East £13,502mn
North West £26,377mn
Yorkshire and the Humber £16,100mn
East Midlands £17,673mn
West Midlands £20,002mn
East £27,437mn
London £35,253mn
South East £42,751mn
South West £12,420mn

Total value of UK exports: £294,501 million

£ million

Northern Ireland £5,712mn
Scotland £17,360mn
Unknown £46,486mn
England £211,514mn
Wales £13,429mn

Source: UK Regional Trade in Goods Statistics: Quarter 4, 2011 Press Release. HM Revenue & Customs. Issued 8 March 2012. Crown copyright 2012.

Threat or opportunity...

Globalisation can be a force for good. It has the potential to generate wealth and improve living standards. But it isn't doing that well at the moment.

The benefits from increased trade, investment and technological innovation are not fairly distributed. The experience of the international trade union movement suggests that the reality for the majority of the world's population is that things are getting worse.

Globalisation as we know it is increasing the gap between rich and poor. This is because the policies that drive the globalisation process are largely focused on the needs of business.

Globalisation can be a force for good. It has the potential to generate wealth and improve living standards. But it isn't doing that well at the moment

The relentless drive to liberalise trade, i.e. to remove trade barriers, promote privatisation, and reduce regulation (including legal protection for workers), has had a negative impact on the lives of millions of people around the world. In addition, many of the poorer countries have been pressured to orientate their economies towards producing exports and to reduce already inadequate spending on public services such as health and education so that they can repay their foreign debt. This has forced even more people into a life of poverty and uncertainty.

The role of governments...

The type of globalisation we are experiencing is sometimes portrayed as an inevitable, technologically-driven process that we must adapt to in order to survive and prosper. For millions of workers, in the developing as well as the developed world, this has been translated into living with greater job insecurity and worse conditions.

TRADES UNION CONGRESS

But the reality is that the globalisation we have seen in recent decades has been driven by a laborious process of international rule-making and enforcement. Governments have made those rules. There has been a conscious political choice to pursue the policies that underpin the process. Of course, domestic, economic, industrial and social policies also play a crucial role in determining living conditions, though poorer countries are less able to resist globalisation due to their economically weaker position.

The key players...

A number of key players are driving globalisation. They include:

⇨ multinational enterprises which carry out business across national boundaries;

⇨ the World Trade Organization (WTO), through which international trade agreements are negotiated and enforced;

⇨ the World Bank and the International Monetary Fund (IMF), which are meant to assist governments in achieving development aims through the provision of loans and technical assistance.

Ways need to be found to manage and structure globalisation so that it supports fundamental human rights and sustainable development, and generates prosperity for ordinary people

They have championed the trade liberalisation policies mentioned above. Governments, and these international institutions, are instrumental in determining the outcome of globalisation.

The impact on women...

The impact of globalisation on men and women is different.

Women, particularly those in developing countries, suffer disproportionately when public services are cut back. This is because they have primary responsibility for caring for children and other family members. Also, girls are more likely to be withdrawn from school when the family income needs to be supplemented or when the cost of education rises.

While the expansion of international trade has generated employment opportunities for women in certain circumstances, trade policies have often served to entrench the traditionally inferior role assigned to women in many countries. Occupational segregation, pay inequality and unequal access to resources are but a

few of the discriminatory measures that women face. The rise of Export Processing Zones, where large numbers of young women labour in poor and dangerous conditions to produce cheap consumer goods, and the expansion of outsourcing and home-based employment, have also raised new issues and concerns for women workers.

Putting people first...

Ways need to be found to manage and structure globalisation so that it supports fundamental human rights and sustainable development, and generates prosperity for ordinary people, particularly the poorest. Left unchecked, globalisation will lead to their further marginalisation and impoverishment.

⇨ The above information is reprinted with kind permission from the Trades Union Congress (TUC). Visit www.tuc.org.uk for more information.

© TUC

Living in an interconnected world

'...the sheer weight of the combined aspirations and lifestyles of 500 million Europeans is just too great. Never mind the legitimate desires of many other billions on our planet to share those lifestyles... We will need to change the behaviour of European consumers. To work on people's awareness and to influence their habits.' Janez Potočnik, European Union Commissioner for Environment (March 2010).

Five years ago Bisie was jungle. Located in the Wailikale territory, east Congo, it is now a cramped township as a result of the discovery of cassiterite, a derivative of tin that is a crucial component in the circuitry of many modern gadgets. It's in your mobile phone, laptop, digital cameras and gaming devices.

Cassiterite is widely sought after and very valuable. Indeed, our demand for consumer electronics has resulted in a price surge for tin ore. Prices on the London Metal Exchange have increased from around US$ 5,000 per tonne in 2003 to more than US$ 26,000 per tonne in late 2010, according to the *Financial Times*.

Our long-standing demand for natural resources to feed, clothe, house, transport and entertain ourselves is accelerating

Today, a range of natural resources in the forests and jungles of the Congo are in great demand. Nevertheless, the Congo remains extremely poor. During the past 15 years more than five million have died in eastern Congo in a war between several armed groups. And it is estimated that no less than 300,000 women have been raped.

This has happened before in the Congo, which was colonised just over 100 years ago by King Leopold II of Belgium. He became one of the richest men in the world by selling rubber from the Congo. This was the time of industrialisation and the booming car industry depended on rubber.

Our long-standing demand for natural resources to feed, clothe, house, transport and entertain ourselves is accelerating just as stocks of certain resources are reaching critically low levels.

Natural systems are also subject to new demands, such as for plant-based chemicals or for biomass to replace fossil fuels. Taken together, these mounting demands on a shrinking resource base point to serious risks to Europe's development.

Margot Wallström, UN Secretary-General's Special Representative on Sexual Violence in Conflict, says:

'As global citizens we are all tied to the violence taking place in the Congo. The extraction of conflict minerals that sustains this conflict connects us all.'

Development for everyone

'The Millennium Declaration in 2000 was a milestone in international cooperation, inspiring development efforts that have improved the lives of hundreds of millions of people around the world. The eight Millennium Development Goals (MDGs) provide a structure for the entire international community to work together towards a common end.

'The goals are achievable but improvements in the lives of the poor have been unacceptably slow, and some hard-won gains are being eroded by the climate, food and economic crises.

'The world possesses the resources and knowledge to ensure that even the poorest countries and others held back by disease, geographic isolation or civil strife can be empowered to achieve the MDGs. Meeting the goals is everyone's business. Falling short would multiply the dangers of our world – from instability to epidemic diseases to environmental degradation. But achieving the goals will put us on a fast track to a world that is more stable, more just, and more secure.'

Ban Ki-moon, Secretary General, United Nations, says in *The Millennium Development Goals Report 2010* (UN, 2010):

'Billions of people are looking to the international community to realise the great vision embodied in the Millennium Declaration. Let us keep that promise.'

Europe and the new balance of power

As the 21st century progresses we see that more and more key global dynamics are outside Europe's influence and control. This has implications in terms of access to resources.

Globally, we see marked uncertainty regarding supply and access to a range of crucial natural resources: food, water and fuels. Europe's need for resources could in coming decades be matched by those of China, India, Brazil and others, putting even greater pressure on the environment.

EUROPEAN ENVIRONMENT AGENCY

Indeed, some developing nations are racing towards levels of economic activity equal to Europe's: their populations, consumption levels and production capacity have the potential to dwarf ours. Their legitimate quest to develop economically and socially will lead to greater use of global stocks of raw materials. China in particular is proving adept at securing access to raw materials from a range of countries and regions.

The human population is growing, technologies are advancing and the power of non-governmental private actors such as multinationals is expanding. In the context of weak international governance mechanisms, these forces threaten a global 'free for all' in securing and accessing natural resources.

Globalisation: a framework for human development

The very nature of globalisation also provides opportunities and structures for a different outcome. The seeds exist for effective, fair global governance of matters critical to us all.

The United Nations' Millennium Development Goals are just one example of a global policy process devoted to equitable and sustainable human development.

International climate talks have made progress over the past year. The Cancún Agreement, signed in December 2010, acknowledges for the first time in a United Nations document that global warming must be kept below 2°C compared to the pre-industrial temperature.

The agreement confirms that developed countries – whose industrial activities and footprint initiated man-made climate change – will mobilise US$ 100 billion in climate funding for developing countries annually by 2020. It also establishes a Green Climate Fund through which much of the funding will be channelled.

Innovations such as the so-called 'REDD+' (Reducing Emissions from Deforestation and Forest Degradation) mechanism enable action to reduce emissions from deforestation and forest degradation in developing countries. None of these activities would be possible without global governance structures and a spirit of cooperation.

The European Union is seeking to promote collaborative responses to common challenges and goals. The EU's *2020 Vision* sets out a strategy for growth designed around a smart, sustainable and inclusive economy.

A growing role for non-state actors

Global political processes clearly have an important role to play in ensuring that economic growth doesn't destroy the underlying natural systems. But another defining characteristic of globalisation is the growing importance of non-government actors.

Multinational businesses, such as mobile phone and IT companies, can also play a key role in delivering sustainable development. The first company to certify their products as free of 'conflict' minerals will have a positive impact on many lives and massive marketing potential.

We must take the innovative research and development examples of leading companies and apply them to the challenges facing us. We must mobilise the full range of problem-solving capacity available to us towards continued, sustainable development.

Global political processes clearly have an important role to play in ensuring that economic growth doesn't destroy the underlying natural systems

As citizens – individually and through non-governmental organisations – we are also mobilising. Some of us take to the streets to protest. Some are investing their time and energy in rediscovering food or community activism. Many are adjusting their consumption choices to minimise environmental impacts and ensure a fair return for producers in developing countries. The point is: globalisation is affecting all of us and we're beginning to wake up to the fact that we are not powerless: we can shape things.

Develop, create, work and educate

We must continue to develop, to create, to work and educate ourselves, and become smarter about our use of natural resources. For example, the first, critical aim of the Millennium Development Goals is to secure the natural environment on which the poorest of the poor depend for their daily survival.

This means managing natural resources in a way that allows local communities to survive, then benefit and then advance. This is one of the major challenges facing us globally.

It's a challenge in which Europeans have a large part to play. Managing global resources sustainably will be key to equitable economic prosperity, greater social cohesion and a healthier environment.

5 July 2011

⇨ The above information is reprinted with kind permission from the European Environment Agency. Visit www.eea.europa.eu for more information.

© European Environment Agency

Debt

Information from CAFOD.

What is debt?

Most of us have to borrow a large amount of money at some time in our lives. Buying a house usually involves taking on debt in the form of a mortgage. For many people, their first debt is their student loan. The sum borrowed is called the principal. On top of the principal you have to pay interest – the fee charged by the lender to the borrower for the use of the lender's money.

How do countries get into debt?

All countries have to borrow money from time to time. Just as house buyers borrow money which they pay back over many years, poorer countries use loans to finance basic infrastructure like dams and road systems.

Developing countries and debt

In the 1970s, rich oil-producing countries put their massive profits into banks to earn interest. To pay this interest, the banks made loans to developing countries. Interest rates were low, and these loans were thought to be affordable. It hardly mattered what the loans were used for because the borrowing governments guaranteed the debt. This is called 'sovereign debt'.

The causes of the crisis

Between 1979 and 1982, interest rates more than doubled worldwide, dramatically raising the cost of loans. The US dollar appreciated in value against other currencies. Loans were made in US dollars, and therefore became much more expensive, as loans were also paid back in US dollars.

At the same time, a worldwide recession reduced demand for developing countries' key exports, like coffee, cocoa and copper – and prices for these exports fell dramatically. Developing countries were earning much less income, but having to pay much more for their loans.

Try this

Go to www.un.org/millenniumgoals and find out what Millennium Goal 8 says about debt. Do you think the debt target has been achieved?

Fact

Developing countries spend $1.5 billion every day on debt repayments. $34 million of this is paid by the very poorest countries. (Jubilee Debt Campaign, 2010)

Try this

What would you do if you owed someone money and were finding it hard to repay?

What difference do you think being in debt has made to developing countries? Do you think they would be different today if they hadn't been in debt?

Fact

In 2008 the total debt owed abroad by all developing countries was $3.7 trillion, with some $600 billion paid back to developed countries and their institutions in that year alone.

Try this

Debate the statement: 'Developing countries shouldn't have their debt cancelled – once you take out a loan you have to pay it back.'

Some countries are refusing to pay back some debts. Why do you think this is?

Fact

For every $1 developing countries receive from developed countries in aid, $5 is returned in debt repayments. (Jubilee Debt Campaign)

Impact of debt

Having become much more expensive, the debts became unmanageable. Countries took out more loans to pay off their original debts. These new loans mostly came from the World Bank, but were conditional – they came with strings attached. Borrowing governments had to show that they were committed to paying off their loans, by cutting public spending on things like education and health. The money saved would then be paid towards the debt. But poorly-educated and unhealthy populations would never be able to pay off the debt. Debt was keeping poor countries poor.

Debt cancellation

In the early 1980s, the World Bank launched a series of initiatives to help alleviate the poverty and debt caused by huge loans. At first, these were just new loans, with lower rates of interest and longer repayment periods. When these did not work, they launched the Heavily Indebted Poor Countries initiative (HIPC). This was a

promise to cancel debt, on the condition that indebted countries made a number of economic and social reforms. Following criticism that HIPC did not cancel enough debt in enough countries, the Multilateral Debt Initiative was launched in 2005, which sped up debt cancellation by 100 per cent.

However, the vast majority of poor countries have not had their debt cancelled, and are still heavily indebted. Many countries are not able to satisfy the conditions for debt cancellation.

It's estimated that although around $100 billion in debt has been cancelled, another $400 billion of debt cancellation is necessary if 100 countries are to meet their people's basic needs (Jubilee Debt Campaign).

Haiti: debt and disaster

In January 2010, a massive earthquake struck Haiti, one of the poorest countries in the world. The country was devastated. Over 200,000 people died and many more were injured.

Haiti was part of the HIPC programme but still owed many millions in debt. It was clear that the little money Haiti had was needed for rebuilding. After campaigning by CAFOD and other organisations, international financial institutions, like the World Bank and the IMF, agreed to cancel Haiti's remaining debt. Over $700 million that would have flowed out of the country could now be used for the recovery. After Haiti's earthquake, the Post-Catastrophe Debt Relief Trust Fund was set up. Following a major disaster, this fund can be used by poor countries to reduce, or in some cases, cancel, their debt payments.

The money lenders

Multilateral lending: When international organisations, such as the World Bank and the International Monetary Fund (IMF), and regional development banks like the African Development Bank give loans to countries.

Bilateral lending: When one government lends money directly to another government.

Commercial lending: When banks and private companies give loans to countries.

Making a difference

Debt cancellation makes a real difference to developing countries. According to the World Bank, countries that benefited from HIPC increased their social spending by an average of 45 per cent between 1999 and 2003. Budgets for healthcare and schools increased dramatically:

⇨ Zambia – people in poor rural areas no longer have to pay for healthcare.

⇨ Uganda and Tanzania – primary school fees abolished, resulting in huge increases in attendance.

⇨ Malawi – teacher training programme established with thousands of new teachers trained every year.

The vast majority of poor countries have not had their debt cancelled, and are still heavily indebted. Many countries are not able to satisfy the conditions for debt cancellation

What CAFOD thinks

Advances being made by countries that have had their debts cancelled shows that debt cancellation helps countries to escape poverty.

Great progress has been made, but the debt issue is still not resolved. Poor countries still need to borrow money to develop. Debts are mounting again. Financial crises often hit poor countries disproportionately more than developed countries, for example by lowering demand for their exports or reducing earnings from tourism, making it difficult for them to keep up loan repayments. Conditions, like cutting public spending, may still be attached to new loans.

CAFOD is a member of the Jubilee Debt Campaign, which believes rich countries need to cancel the remaining unpayable debts of all the world's poor countries. New loans should be fair and not force policies onto developing countries.

Useful websites

Jubilee Debt Campaign: jubileedebtcampaign.org.uk

UN Millennium Development Goals: un.org/millennium goals

World Bank (source of financial and technical assistance to developing countries): worldbank.org

All facts correct May 2011

⇨ The above information is reprinted with kind permission from CAFOD. Visit www.cafod.org.uk for more information.

© CAFOD

Understanding the World Trade Organization

There are a number of ways of looking at the World Trade Organization. It is an organisation for trade opening. It is a forum for governments to negotiate trade agreements. It is a place for them to settle trade disputes. It operates a system of trade rules. Essentially, the WTO is a place where member governments try to sort out the trade problems they face with each other.

Who we are

The WTO was born out of negotiations, and everything the WTO does is the result of negotiations. The bulk of the WTO's current work comes from the 1986–94 negotiations called the Uruguay Round and earlier negotiations under the General Agreement on Tariffs and Trade (GATT). The WTO is currently the host to new negotiations, under the 'Doha Development Agenda' launched in 2001.

Where countries have faced trade barriers and wanted them lowered, the negotiations have helped to open markets for trade. But the WTO is not just about opening markets, and in some circumstances its rules support maintaining trade barriers – for example, to protect consumers or prevent the spread of disease.

TRADE BARRIERS IN ACTION

MUM WON'T LET ME SWAP MY MARBLES FOR YOUR NEW BIKE!

At its heart are the WTO agreements, negotiated and signed by the bulk of the world's trading nations. These documents provide the legal ground rules for international commerce. They are essentially contracts, binding governments to keep their trade policies within agreed limits. Although negotiated and signed by governments, the goal is to help producers of goods and services, exporters and importers conduct their business, while allowing governments to meet social and environmental objectives.

Where countries have faced trade barriers and wanted them lowered, the negotiations have helped to open markets for trade. But the WTO is not just about opening markets, and in some circumstances its rules support maintaining trade barriers

The system's overriding purpose is to help trade flow as freely as possible – so long as there are no undesirable side effects – because this is important for economic development and wellbeing. That partly means removing obstacles. It also means ensuring that individuals, companies and governments know what the trade rules are around the world, and giving them the confidence that there will be no sudden changes of policy. In other words, the rules have to be 'transparent' and predictable.

Trade relations often involve conflicting interests. Agreements, including those painstakingly negotiated in the WTO system, often need interpreting. The most harmonious way to settle these differences is through some neutral procedure based on an agreed legal foundation. That is the purpose behind the dispute settlement process written into the WTO agreements.

What we do

The WTO is run by its member governments. All major decisions are made by the membership as a whole, either by ministers (who usually meet at least once every two years) or by their ambassadors or delegates (who meet regularly in Geneva).

While the WTO is driven by its member states, it could not function without its Secretariat to coordinate the activities. The Secretariat employs over 600 staff, and its experts – lawyers, economists, statisticians and communications experts – assist WTO members on a daily basis to ensure, among other things, that negotiations progress smoothly, and that the rules of international trade are correctly applied and enforced.

WTO agreements require governments to make their trade policies transparent by notifying the WTO about laws in force and measures adopted

Trade negotiations

The WTO agreements cover goods, services and intellectual property. They spell out the principles of liberalisation, and the permitted exceptions. They include individual countries' commitments to lower customs tariffs and other trade barriers, and to open and keep open services markets. They set procedures for settling disputes. These agreements are not static; they are renegotiated from time to time and new agreements can be added to the package. Many are now being negotiated under the Doha Development Agenda, launched by WTO trade ministers in Doha, Qatar, in November 2001.

Implementation and monitoring

WTO agreements require governments to make their trade policies transparent by notifying the WTO about laws in force and measures adopted. Various WTO councils and committees seek to ensure that these requirements are being followed and that WTO agreements are being properly implemented. All WTO members must undergo periodic scrutiny of their trade policies and practices, each review containing reports by the country concerned and the WTO Secretariat.

Dispute settlement

The WTO's procedure for resolving trade quarrels under the Dispute Settlement Understanding is vital for enforcing the rules and therefore for ensuring that trade flows smoothly. Countries bring disputes to the WTO if they think their rights under the agreements are being infringed. Judgements by specially appointed independent experts are based on interpretations of the agreements and individual countries' commitments.

Building trade capacity

WTO agreements contain special provision for developing countries, including longer time periods to implement agreements and commitments, measures to increase their trading opportunities, and support to help them build their trade capacity, to handle disputes and to implement technical standards. The WTO organises hundreds of technical cooperation missions to developing countries annually. It also holds numerous courses each year in Geneva for government officials. Aid for Trade aims to help developing countries develop the skills and infrastructure needed to expand their trade.

Outreach

The WTO maintains regular dialogue with non-governmental organisations, parliamentarians, other international organisations, the media and the general public on various aspects of the WTO and the ongoing Doha negotiations, with the aim of enhancing cooperation and increasing awareness of WTO activities.

WTO agreements contain special provision for developing countries, including longer time periods to implement... commitments

Fact file

Location: Geneva, Switzerland

Established: 1 January 1995

Created by: Uruguay Round negotiations (1986–94)

Membership: 153 countries on 10 February 2011

Budget: 196 million Swiss francs for 2011

Secretariat staff: 640

Head: Pascal Lamy (Director-General)

Functions:

⇨ Administering WTO trade agreements

⇨ Forum for trade negotiations

⇨ Handling trade disputes

⇨ Monitoring national trade policies

⇨ Technical assistance and training for developing countries

⇨ Cooperation with other international organisations

⇨ The above information is reprinted with kind permission from the World Trade Organization. It originally appeared on their website here: /www.wto.org/english/thewto_e/whatis_e/who_we_are_e.htm. Visit www.wto.org for more information.

© World Trade Organization

What is the World Bank?

In 2004 the World Bank provided $20.1 billion for 245 projects in developing countries worldwide, with its finance and/or technical expertise aimed at helping those countries reduce poverty.

We live in a world so rich that global income is more than $31 trillion a year. In this world, the average person in some countries earns more than $40,000 a year. But in this same world, 2.8 billion people – more than half the people in developing countries – live on less than $700 a year. Of these, 1.2 billion earn less than $1 a day.

As a result, 33,000 children die every day in developing countries. In these countries, each minute more than one woman dies during childbirth. Poverty keeps more than 100 million children, most of them girls, out of school.

The challenge of reducing these levels of poverty, while the population continues to grow – by an estimated three billion people over the next 50 years – is enormous.

The World Bank works to bridge this divide and turn rich country resources into poor country growth. One of the world's largest sources of development assistance, the World Bank supports the efforts of developing country governments to build schools and health centres, provide water and electricity, fight disease, and protect the environment.

Not a bank, but rather a specialised agency

The World Bank is not a 'bank' in the common sense. It is one of the United Nations' specialised agencies, and is made up of 184 member countries. These countries are jointly responsible for how the institution is financed and how its money is spent. Along with the rest of the development community, the World Bank centres its efforts on reaching the Millennium Development Goals, agreed to by UN members in 2000 and aimed at sustainable poverty reduction.

The 'World Bank' is the name that has come to be used for the International Bank for Reconstruction and Development (IBRD) and the International Development Association (IDA). Together these organisations provide low-interest loans, interest-free credit and grants to developing countries.

Some 10,000 development professionals from nearly every country in the world work in the World Bank's Washington DC headquarters or in its 109 country offices.

$9 billion in assistance

The world's low-income countries generally cannot borrow money in international markets or can only do so at high interest rates. In addition to direct contributions and loans from developed countries, these countries receive grants, interest-free loans and technical assistance from the World Bank to enable them to provide basic services. In the case of the loans, countries have 35 to 40 years to repay, with a ten-year grace period.

In fiscal 2004 IDA provided $9 billion in financing for 158 projects in 62 low-income countries.

Interest-free credit and grant financing comes from IDA, the world's largest source of concessional assistance. Some 40 rich countries provide the money for this funding by making contributions every four years. The fund was replenished most recently in 2002, with nearly $9 billion from donors and another $6.6 billion from the Bank's resources. At that time, donors agreed on increased use of IDA grants – up to 21 per cent of resources – to help address the special difficulties, such as the HIV/AIDS epidemic, faced by the poorest and most vulnerable countries.

IDA credits make up about one-quarter of the Bank's financial assistance. Aside from IDA funds, very little of the Bank's income is provided by its member countries.

$11 billion in loans

Higher-income developing countries – some of which can borrow from commercial sources, but generally only at very high interest rates – receive loans from the IBRD.

Countries that borrow from the IBRD have more time to repay than if they borrowed from a commercial bank – 15 to 20 years with a three-to-five-year grace period before the repayment of principal begins. Developing country governments borrow money for specific programmes, including poverty reduction efforts, delivery of social services, protection of the environment and promotion of economic growth that will improve living standards. In fiscal 2004 IBRD provided loans totalling $11 billion in support of 87 projects in 33 countries.

Raising capital

The IBRD raises almost all its money in the world's financial markets – $13 billion in fiscal 2004. With a AAA credit rating, it issues bonds to raise money and then passes on the low interest rates to its borrowers.

The World Bank Group

In addition to IBRD and IDA, three other organisations make up the World Bank Group. The International Finance Corporation (IFC) promotes private sector investment by supporting high-risk sectors and countries. The Multilateral Investment Guarantee Agency (MIGA) provides political risk insurance (guarantees) to investors in and lenders to developing countries. And the International Centre for Settlement of Investment Disputes (ICSID) settles investment disputes between foreign investors and their host countries.

Global goods

Over the past few years, the World Bank has put significant resources into activities meant to have global impact. One is debt relief, and under the enhanced Heavily Indebted Poor Countries (HIPC) Initiative, 26 poor countries have received debt relief which will save them $41 billion over time. The money these countries save in debt repayments will instead be put into housing, education, health and welfare programmes for the poor.

The World Bank, along with 189 countries and numerous organisations, has committed to an unprecedented global partnership to fight poverty. The Millennium Development Goals define specific targets in terms of school enrolments, child mortality, maternal health, disease and access to water to be met by 2015.

Among numerous other global partnerships, the World Bank has put supporting the fight against HIV/AIDS at the top of its agenda. It is the world's largest long-term financer of HIV/AIDS programmes. Current Bank commitments for HIV/AIDS amount to more than $1.3 billion, with half of that for sub-Saharan Africa.

Corruption and fraud

The World Bank works with countries in their anti-corruption efforts and also has a number of mechanisms in place to prevent corruption and fraud in bank-financed projects. The Department of Institutional Integrity has a 24-hour Fraud and Corruption Hotline: 1-800-831-0463.

The variety of work on the ground

The Bank is currently involved in more than 1,800 projects in virtually every sector and developing country. These are as diverse as providing microcredit in Bosnia Herzegovina and raising AIDS awareness in communities in Guinea, supporting education of girls in Bangladesh and improving health care delivery in Mexico, helping East Timor rebuild upon independence or India to rebuild Gujarat after a devastating earthquake.

In addition to a small selection of project profiles, the Countries and Projects sections of the World Bank's website provide details of the Bank's work on the ground.

Ten things you never knew about the World Bank

The World Bank...

1 is the largest external funder of education...

2 and of HIV/AIDS programmes;

3 is a leader in the anti-corruption effort;

4 strongly supports debt relief;

5 is one of the largest funders of biodiversity projects;

6 works with partners;

7 helps bring clean water, electricity and transport to the poor;

8 involves civil society in every aspect of its work;

9 helps countries emerging from conflict;

10 is responding to the voices of poor people.

⇨ The above information is reprinted with kind permission from the World Bank. Visit http://web. worldbank.org for more information on this and other related topics.

© World Bank

WORLD BANK

The International Monetary Fund (IMF)

What we do.

With its near-global membership of 187 countries, the IMF is uniquely placed to help member governments take advantage of the opportunities – and manage the challenges – posed by globalisation and economic development more generally. The IMF tracks global economic trends and performance, alerts its member countries when it sees problems on the horizon, provides a forum for policy dialogue, and passes on know-how to governments on how to tackle economic difficulties.

The IMF provides policy advice and financing to members in economic difficulties and also works with developing nations to help them achieve macroeconomic stability and reduce poverty.

Marked by massive movements of capital and abrupt shifts in comparative advantage, globalisation affects countries' policy choices in many areas, including labour, trade and tax policies. Helping a country benefit from globalisation while avoiding potential downsides is an important task for the IMF. The global economic crisis has highlighted just how interconnected countries have become in today's world economy.

Key IMF activities

The IMF supports its membership by providing:

⇨ policy advice to governments and central banks based on analysis of economic trends and cross-country experiences;

⇨ research, statistics, forecasts and analysis based on tracking of global, regional, and individual economies and markets;

⇨ loans to help countries overcome economic difficulties;

⇨ concessional loans to help fight poverty in developing countries; and

⇨ technical assistance and training to help countries improve the management of their economies.

Original aims

The IMF was founded more than 60 years ago toward the end of World War II. The founders aimed to build a framework for economic cooperation that would avoid a repetition of the disastrous economic policies that had contributed to the Great Depression of the 1930s and the global conflict that followed.

Since then the world has changed dramatically, bringing extensive prosperity and lifting millions out of poverty, especially in Asia. In many ways the IMF's main purpose – to provide the global public good of financial stability – is the same today as it was when the organisation was established. More specifically, the IMF continues to:

⇨ provide a forum for cooperation on international monetary problems;

⇨ facilitate the growth of international trade, thus promoting job creation, economic growth and poverty reduction;

⇨ promote exchange rate stability and an open system of international payments; and

⇨ lend countries foreign exchange when needed, on a temporary basis and under adequate safeguards, to help them address balance of payments problems.

An adapting IMF

The IMF has evolved along with the global economy throughout its 65-year history, allowing the organisation to retain its central role within the international financial architecture.

As the world economy struggles to restore growth and jobs after the worst crisis since the Great Depression, the IMF has emerged as a very different institution. During the crisis, it mobilised on many fronts to support its member countries. It increased its lending, used its cross-country experience to advise on policy solutions,

INTERNATIONAL MONETARY FUND

supported global policy coordination and reformed the way it makes decisions. The result is an institution that is more in tune with the needs of its 187 member countries.

⇨ **Stepping up crisis lending.** The IMF responded quickly to the global economic crisis, with lending commitments reaching a record level of more than US$250 billion in 2010. This figure includes a sharp increase in concessional lending (that's to say, subsidised lending at rates below those being charged by the market) to the world's poorest nations.

⇨ **Greater lending flexibility.** The IMF has overhauled its lending framework to make it better suited to countries' individual needs. It is also working with other regional institutions to create a broader financial safety net, which could help prevent new crises.

⇨ **Providing analysis and advice.** The IMF's monitoring, forecasts and policy advice, informed by a global perspective and by experience from previous

crises, have been in high demand and have been used by the G20.

⇨ **Drawing lessons from the crisis.** The IMF is contributing to the ongoing effort to draw lessons from the crisis for policy, regulation and reform of the global financial architecture.

⇨ **Historic reform of governance.** The IMF's member countries also agreed to a significant increase in the voice of dynamic emerging and developing economies in the decision-making of the institution, while preserving the voice of the low-income members.

⇨ The above information is reprinted with kind permission from the International Monetary Fund (IMF). Visit www.imf.org for more information.

© International Monetary Fund

Globalisation and identity

By Pascal Lamy, Director-General of the World Trade Organization (WTO).

Is globalisation, which is shaping our societies whether we like it or not, a threat to identity? If we were to believe all that we hear, the winds of globalisation are wreaking havoc everywhere, uprooting identities and cultures which for centuries have been shaping human relations, sweeping away all local values and customs, and leaving behind an irretrievably flat wasteland, to use Thomas Friedman's well known metaphor. According to this view, globalisation is a sort of homogenisation that is sapping our strength and causing us to decline.

There are plenty of examples to illustrate this widespread view. Thanks to the spectacular development of transportation and new information technologies, our planet has apparently become a village whose inhabitants are developing increasingly similar lifestyles and consumption patterns. In Paris, Brasilia, Shanghai or Montreal, the same restaurant and clothing chains are invading the shopping districts, the same films are flooding the cinemas, and the same music has taken over the radio waves. There is not a single place in the world, however remote, where you cannot find a bottle of Coke or Pepsi to quench your thirst.

This globalisation, often seen as a pervasive homogenising force which threatens the enormous diversity of identities that contributes so much to the world we live in, appears to be provoking a sudden reassertion of identity as a counter-reaction to the perceived domination of one culture over another, depriving us of what makes each one of us unique. In a world where

physical boundaries are disappearing, swept away by the wave of technology, identification with a place or a group becomes the only refuge against the threat of uniformity, the only remaining bastion of diversity.

Is the revival of nationalism, the emergence or resurgence of political movements defending national, ethnic or religious identity, not concrete proof of this trend? It is as if the thirst for inclusion could only be quenched by exclusion.

The question is a perfectly legitimate one. It is indeed tempting to interpret these events as a 'clash of civilisations', to quote the well known phrase of Samuel Huntington.

But is there really a clash? Do globalisation and identity belong to two different and diametrically opposed universes? When it comes to new information technologies, capital movements, the opening up of trade, and the increasingly globalised production chains that go hand in hand with economic globalisation, borders and proximity no longer count. Identity, on the other hand, has its roots in a location, in history, in culture, in values, in a language, or in a belief. Globalisation means movement, perpetual change, while identity means roots. Identity is sedentary while technological progress is nomadic.

4 November 2010

⇨ Information from the World Trade Organization. This is an extract from a speech given by Pascal Lamy, the full text of which can be found here: www.wto.org/english/news_e/sppl_e/sppl178_e.htm

© World Trade Organization

Frequently asked questions on globalisation, free trade, the WTO and NAMA

Information from Friends of the Earth.

Globalisation

What is globalisation?

Globalisation is a term to explain the increased social and trade-related exchanges between nations. It implies that nations are moving closer together economically and culturally. In recent years, through the Internet, air travel, trade and popular culture, globalisation has rapidly increased.

Increased interaction between nations through globalisation must be a good thing?

There is no doubt globalisation has brought many benefits, exotic holidays, solidarity and information-sharing to name a few. However, it is important to remember there are negative aspects too: for example, indigenous customs and languages are disappearing and small local businesses and farms are being swallowed up by large multinationals. Globalisation also has environmental implications such as increased air travel or tourist pressures on remote and delicate ecosystems. Handled properly and in a sustainable manner, Friends of the Earth considers globalisation a positive thing.

Free trade

What is the problem with trade?

Trade itself is not necessarily a problem; trade, after all, has been around for centuries and has been an important driver in redistributing wealth and achieving growth in the world economy. Friends of the Earth is not against trade, but against the current system of corporate-driven 'free' trade.

What is 'free' trade?

'Free' trade is an economic theory which encourages the unhindered movement of goods and services between countries. 'Free' trade supporters view import or export taxes, quotas and subsidies, and national preferences to trade with certain countries or only in certain products, such as only importing shrimps caught in turtle-friendly nets, to be hindrances which therefore should be eliminated.

What is liberalisation?

Liberalisation refers to a relaxation of previous government restrictions, usually in areas of social or economic policy, in pursuit of the 'free' trade model. Liberalising trade involves taking down the 'barriers' discussed above.

Why not get rid of taxes, if it makes goods more expensive?

Import and export taxes to regulate the trade in products have been around for years. For example, the UK grew rich taxing imports on Indian cloths while we protected our own textile industry. Besides generating income for governments, taxes are an important instrument to regulate economically and environmentally damaging products coming into and leaving a country.

Economically it is important to prevent cheaper goods putting national industries out of business. This is particularly important for developing countries who face cheap imports from wealthier nations with more established industries. Taxation particularly helps weaker economies, where war, colonisation or a country's geography and size have meant they are less economically developed than their competitors. For example, countries that are only able to grow one type of crop due to their climate must be allowed to give support to the farmers whose livelihood depends on growing it.

Environmentally, taxes can restrict the use of products which are damaging to the environment. Products that come into the country, for example cars which use a lot of fuel and emit carbon dioxide, or products which may leave the country, like rare types of wood such as mahogany, often have an environmental impact.

Although cheaper goods may appear to be preferable to the consumer, the long-term costs outweigh any benefits of a properly regulated trade system. It is also important to remember that the big winners from a tax-free trade system are big business, not consumers. Governments must be able to use such measures and adapt their economic policies to protect their people and the environment.

By dismissing 'free' trade we deny jobs for people in less developed countries

There are a number of problems with this idea. Jobs created through 'free' trade, including in developing countries, tend increasingly to be low paid, with long hours that damage health and prevent workers from unionising to protect important rights, such as maternity leave or minimum wages. Furthermore, large multinational companies which predominate in 'free' trade don't actually generate the levels of employment that small and medium-sized enterprises do. Multinational corporations control over 33% of the world's productive assets and

over 70% of world trade, but only account for 5% of the world's employment. Also, multinational companies who employ large numbers of people in a single country can increasingly dictate employment terms to the host nation. This means that large companies often threaten to move (and often do move) elsewhere if they think that the weaker environmental or labour standards of another country will help reduce their costs. This phenomenon is often called the race to the bottom.

'Free' trade brings people out of poverty

Friends of the Earth's research shows that in fact 'free' trade has increased poverty between and within countries all over the world. The idea that as the world gets richer, so will the poor is one the rich and powerful have pushed for decades because they stand to gain from increased profits. In fact, despite their rhetoric, rich countries tend to follow 'free' trade theory only when they are certain to benefit. So, while demanding that poor countries remove trade 'barriers', rich countries continue to subsidise and protect their own industries and farmers. 'Free' trade has not worked, millions remain trapped in poverty with little hope of escape. It is the institutions, conditions and rules of international trade, more than anything else, that keep poor people poor.

You're against economic growth

It's obvious that sustainable societies need strong, healthy economies, but that doesn't mean we need to put economic growth above everything else. Economic growth should not be chased at the expense of local businesses, health, employment and the environment – as it is at the moment. Economic growth has costs, and Friends of the Earth wants to see those costs properly accounted for in deciding how we define economic progress.

The only alternative to 'free' trade is protectionism, and I'm against protectionism

It is important not to polarise the argument. Old-style economic protectionism – closing and protecting markets – is not the only alternative. We need to take a much more sophisticated approach to economics, for instance by not measuring progress simply by looking for increases in gross domestic product (GDP).

Why is GDP a bad measure for a country's living standards?

GDP is not the best way to measure economic growth, as it fails to measure quality of life, social progress, poverty eradication, environmental quality, or the social and environmental costs of any money made (for example, cutting down forests people rely on for food, shelter and medicine in order to export the wood to a paper company). These need to be taken into consideration when assessing a country's progress.

'Free' trade has given us a much wider choice of things to buy

In some ways globalisation has increased choice in the shops, but the WTO (see below) rules restrict choices a consumer can make overall. There is a considerable question, for example, about using a precautionary approach to trade in order to protect the environment or health, for instance in the current WTO dispute over GM food and farming. There are also threats in the WTO to governments' ability to ban or label products they believe are potentially harmful, ethically unacceptable or produced in an unacceptable or unsustainable way.

World Trade Organization

What is the WTO or World Trade Organization?

The WTO sets and polices the rules of trade between nations. It promotes increasing 'free' trade through negotiations between its member countries. What is decided in WTO talks has ramifications across the world from rural cotton farmers to people like you and me, the UK consumer.

The WTO has set up committees to ensure that the environment is adequately taken care of

The WTO has set up the Committee on Trade and the Environment (the CTE), but is has proved far from adequate. Despite assurances that the WTO does not inhibit environmental protection, in practice environmental rules are brushed aside if they get in the way of 'free' trade and its associated profits.

The WTO is democratic – every country gets a vote on trade decisions

In theory yes, but the negotiations that lead to those votes and the system itself operate in a climate of intimidation, power games and horse trading. Tit for tat wrangling by countries ('we'll drop our farming subsidies if you let us buy your health service') means that decision-making, particularly for smaller countries, is at best done under duress. Threats to aid packages if countries vote the 'wrong' way are not unheard of. Also, negotiations and disputes cost vast amounts of money and large contingents of staff, lawyers and negotiators. Countries with little money are not able to participate on an equal level with rich countries.

Threats and bullying – for years, rich countries, and the international institutions they control, such as the World Trade Organization, the International Monetary Fund and the World Bank, have been quietly forcing poor countries to follow their economic 'advice'. Through a mixture of persuasion, threats, bullying and conditions attached to loans and aid, poor countries are being forced to open their markets to foreign competition, to

FRIENDS OF THE EARTH

stop helping their vulnerable producers and to privatise essential services, even though there is increasing evidence that such measures will not lead to real, lasting poverty reduction.

Double standards – rich countries often claim to support 'free' trade. They say 'free' trade is the way to sustainable development for all. In fact, despite their rhetoric, rich countries tend to follow 'free' trade theory only when they are certain to benefit. So whilst demanding that poor countries remove trade 'barriers', rich countries continue to subsidise and protect their own industries and farmers.

What's the alternative?

We need a radical change in the agenda, but there is no one-size-fits-all solution to trade. Trade can play a role in poverty reduction and maintaining the environment, but only if balanced by strategic government intervention that strengthens the weakest and serves the poor. Poor country governments must retain the right to choose their own economic policies, including trade policies that work to reduce poverty for the long term. They need the freedom to help support and protect their vulnerable producers, enterprises and traders in the most appropriate way, until they are strong enough to compete. Historically, no country has ever become rich without this kind of intervention.

What do Friends of the Earth want done about 'free' trade?

Friends of the Earth are calling for the WTO negotiations to be halted, and that:

⇨ the WTO must not be used to lower hard-won environmental and social standards;

⇨ full impact assessments must be conducted in all areas and the results properly integrated into any future negotiations; and

⇨ sensitive areas, like fish and forests, must be removed from negotiations altogether.

NAMA

What is NAMA?

The World Trade Organization members negotiate on many different areas in order to increase liberalisation. Agriculture and public services (GATS) are two of the more well known areas. Another is called non-agricultural market access (NAMA). These negotiations aim to remove 'barriers' to 'free' trade in all industrial goods and natural resources. For example, NAMA seeks to take down import tariffs, which make imported goods more expensive. There are also talks about removing other types of trade restrictions known as non-tariff barriers (NTBs), like minimum product standards, product labelling

and product testing, including hard-won environmental and social protections that have taken decades to enact.

Why is NAMA bad for the environment?

In NAMA, all natural resources are effectively on the table for either partial or complete liberalisation, with a particular focus at the moment on fish and fish products, forest products, gems and minerals. This will lead to an increase in their extraction, production and use both legally and illegally, which is bad for the environment and the communities reliant on them for their livelihoods. NTBs which are due to be abolished include measures designed to protect the environment.

Removing NTBs could mean governments being forced to get rid of national measures to:

⇨ certify sustainable wood products;

⇨ label dolphin-friendly tuna;

⇨ enforce building codes and safety fire standards;

⇨ label the ingredients of medicines;

⇨ label the energy efficiency of products;

⇨ encourage recycling.

What is your problem with NAMA?

Friends of the Earth is concerned that governments' ability to protect the environment is threatened by the NAMA talks. Friends of the Earth, along with many campaign groups and trade unions, is concerned about the potential negative impacts of the NAMA talks on poverty, local industries, employment and the environment, both in the industrialised and developing world.

FRIENDS OF THE EARTH

For example, removing tariffs in sensitive areas like 'forest products' will have devastating impacts not only on the people reliant on forests for their livelihoods but also for the environment in terms of biodiversity and combating climate change.

What are Friends of the Earth doing about NAMA?

Friends of the Earth are campaigning against NAMA in a number of areas. Here in the UK we are focusing on its impacts on forests. We have designed a range of materials to get this message across. We are also in communication with government ministers so they are aware of the problems and solutions, as well as the media.

Forest facts

Increased trade in forest products which will lead to deforestation due to NAMA is bad because:

⇨ A single acre of rainforest can contain as many different plant species as the entire UK – some 1,500 species.

⇨ Forests slow climate change by storing 46% of all land-based carbon.

⇨ One billion of the world's poorest people rely on forests to survive.

⇨ Information from Friends of the Earth. Visit www.foe. co.uk for more.

© Friends of the Earth

2012 could see Globalisation 2.0 take off

A greener, more equitable and wellbeing-orientated form of globalisation could be on the horizon, says Dax Lovegrove.

It is looking grim next year, with austerity set to stay, but perhaps this will jump start 'Globalisation 2.0' – a greener, more equitable and wellbeing-orientated form of globalisation. Am I a hopeless optimist? Well, quite possibly, but activities this year show that we could be moving in the right direction.

First off, revolution is already here. The Occupy movement, the UK summer riots and the Arab Spring may not present a clearly defined set of motives, but they do indicate a growing intolerance of the rich-poor divide and the excesses in the more affluent parts of society.

And then there's the Government revisiting a happiness index, further highlighting the flaws with our current preoccupation with GDP. Wellbeing indicators used by the Government and the Office for National Statistics including 'health', 'what we do', 'where we live', 'personal finance' and 'education and skills' have already stirred up a great deal of debate, while perhaps also broadening the nation's outlook on how we measure progress in today's society.

Another part of the wellbeing agenda according to the New Economics Foundation is being more connected to people and issues around us, and this is gaining traction with 'Generation C' – the connected generation. This new breed refers mainly to being connected in an online sense to the latest news, music and games. However, Generation C is also giving rise to an explosion of new international entrepreneurial approaches around collaborative consumption within communities that encourage moves from a throwaway society to one that focuses on re-use. Zilok, Ecomodo, Swapstyle.com and NeighbourGoods are among the many social networking enterprises operating in this space and such outfits are racing ahead with greener alternative business models.

On top of this, leaders from big business have been much more vocal on pursuing economic growth in ways that are far smarter than what we've seen in the past and there has been a shift out of peripheral CSR activities, at least among the more enlightened multinationals. Sky's Jeremy Darroch, Unilever's Paul Polman and Kingfisher's Ian Cheshire are among those who are championing new approaches aligned with protecting the world's natural assets. We could see rapid spread of this new thinking throughout the private sector, and, far greater innovation, informed by Generation C and the aforementioned enterprises.

The Durban and Rio conferences are adding to the emerging perfect storm. These summits, the growing dissatisfaction with the current economic system, the greater importance placed on wellbeing, a more connected generation, community-driven entrepreneurial activity and new thinking among business leaders could see Globalisation 2.0 start to take off in 2012.

Dax Lovegrove is head of business and industry at WWF-UK.

6 January 2012

© Guardian News & Media Ltd 2012

Rethinking the global economy: the case for sharing

The basic assumptions about human nature that inform economic and political decision-making are long outdated and fundamentally flawed. By acknowledging our interdependence and common ethical values, we can build a more sustainable, cooperative and inclusive global economy, argue Rajesh Makwana and Adam Parsons.

As the 21st century unfolds, humanity is faced with a stark reality. Following the world stock market crash in 2008, people everywhere are questioning the unbridled greed, selfishness and competition that has driven the dominant economic model for decades. The old obsession with protecting national interests, the drive to maximise profits at all costs, and the materialistic pursuit of economic growth have failed to benefit the world's poor and led to catastrophic consequences for planet earth.

The incidence of hunger is more widespread than ever before in human history, surpassing one billion people in 2009 despite the record harvests of food being reaped in recent years. At least 1.4 billion people live in extreme poverty, a number equivalent to more than four times the population of the United States. One out of every five people does not have access to clean drinking water. More than a billion people lack access to basic health care services, while over a billion people – the majority of them women – lack a basic education. Every week, more than 115,000 people move into a slum somewhere in Africa, Asia or Latin America. Every day, around 50,000 people die needlessly as a result of being denied the essentials of life.

In the face of these immense challenges, international aid has proven largely ineffective, inadequate, and incapable of enabling governments to secure the basic needs of all citizens. Developed countries were cutting back on foreign aid commitments even before the economic downturn, while the agreed aid target of 0.7 per cent of rich countries' GDP has never been met since it was first conceived 40 years ago. The Millennium Development Goals of merely halving the incidence of hunger and extreme poverty, even if reached by 2015, will still leave hundreds of millions of people in a state of undernourishment and deprivation. When several trillion dollars were rapidly summoned to bail out failed banks in late 2008, it became impossible to understand why the governments of rich nations could not afford a fraction of this sum to 'bail out' the world's poor.

The enduring gap between rich and poor, both within and between countries, is a crisis that lies at the heart of our political and economic problems. For decades, 20 per cent of the world population have controlled 80 per cent of the economy and resources. By 2008, more than half of the world's assets were owned by the richest two per cent of adults, while the bottom half of the world adult population owned only one per cent of wealth. The vast discrepancies in living standards between the Global North and South, which provides no basis for a stable and secure future, can only be redressed through a more equitable distribution of resources at the international level. This will require more inclusive structures of global governance and a new economic framework that goes far beyond existing development efforts to reduce poverty, decrease poor country debt and provide overseas aid.

In both the richest and poorest nations, commercialisation has infiltrated every aspect of life and compromised spiritual, ethical and moral values. The globalised consumer culture holds no higher aspiration than the accumulation of material wealth, even though studies have shown that rising income fails to significantly increase an individual's wellbeing once a minimum standard of living is secured. The organisation of society as a competitive struggle for social position through wealth and acquisition has led to rampant individualism and the consequences of crime, disaffection and the disintegration of family and community ties. Yet governments continue to measure success in terms of economic growth, pursuing ever-greater levels of GDP – regardless of the harmful social consequences of a consumption-driven economy.

Although the crises we face are interlinked and multidimensional, the G20 and other rich nations offer no vision of change towards a more sustainable world. The old formula, based on deregulation, privatisation and the liberalisation of trade and finance, was unmasked by the economic crisis and shown to be incapable of promoting lasting human development. Multilateral institutions like the World Bank and International Monetary Fund have failed the world's poor, and the myth that economic growth will eventually benefit all has long been shattered. As we also know, endless growth is unsustainable on a planet with finite resources. This impasse is further compounded by ecological degradation and climate change – the side-effects of economic 'progress' that disproportionately affect the poorest people, who are least to blame for causing these multiple crises.

Humanity's ability to effectively address these interrelated crises requires governments to accept certain fundamental understandings that are instrumental to securing our common future. Firstly, that humankind is part of an extended family that shares the same basic needs and rights, and this must be adequately reflected in the structures and institutions of global governance. And secondly, that many basic assumptions about human nature that inform the thrust of economic decision-making – particularly in industrialised nations – are long outdated and fundamentally flawed. The creation of an inclusive economic framework that reflects our global interdependence requires policy-makers to move beyond the belief that human beings are competitive and individualistic, and to instead accept humanity's innate propensity to cooperate and share. This more holistic understanding of our relationship to each other and the planet transcends nations and cultures, and builds on ethics and values common to faith groups around the world. It also reflects the strong sense of solidarity and internationalism which lies at the heart of the global justice movement.

International unity

The first true political expression of our global unity was embodied in the establishment of the United Nations in 1945. Since then, international laws have been devised to help govern relationships between nations and uphold human rights. Cross-border issues such as climate change, global poverty and conflict are uniting world public opinion and compelling governments to cooperate and plan for our collective future. The globalisation of knowledge and cultures, and the ease with which we can communicate and travel around the world, has further served to unite diverse people in distant countries.

But the fact of our global unity is still not sufficiently expressed in our political and economic structures. The international community has yet to ensure that basic human needs, such as access to staple food, clean water and primary healthcare, are universally secured. This cannot be achieved until nations cooperate more effectively, share their natural and economic resources, and ensure that global governance mechanisms reflect

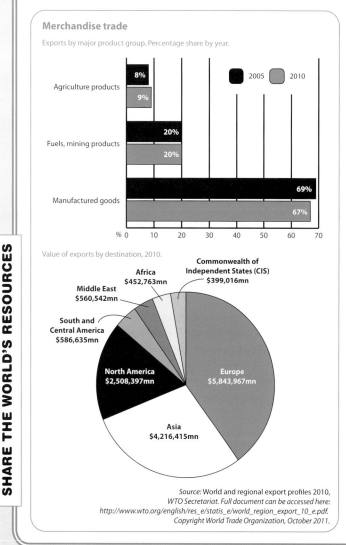

Merchandise trade

Exports by major product group. Percentage share by year.

■ 2005 ▨ 2010

Agriculture products: 8% (2005), 9% (2010)
Fuels, mining products: 20% (2005), 20% (2010)
Manufactured goods: 69% (2005), 67% (2010)

% 0 10 20 30 40 50 60 70

Value of exports by destination, 2010.

Commonwealth of Independent States (CIS) $399,016mn
Africa $452,763mn
Middle East $560,542mn
South and Central America $586,635mn
North America $2,508,397mn
Europe $5,843,967mn
Asia $4,216,415mn

Source: World and regional export profiles 2010, WTO Secretariat. Full document can be accessed here: http://www.wto.org/english/res_e/statis_e/world_region_export_10_e.pdf. Copyright World Trade Organization, October 2011.

and directly support our common needs and rights. At present, the main institutions that govern the global economy are failing to work on behalf of humanity as a whole. In particular, the major bodies that uphold the Bretton Woods mandate (the World Bank, International Monetary Fund and World Trade Organization) are all widely criticised for being undemocratic and furthering the interests of large corporations and rich countries.

A more inclusive international framework urgently needs to be established through the United Nations (UN) and its agencies. Although in need of being significantly strengthened and renewed, the UN is the only multilateral governmental agency with the necessary experience and resources to coordinate the process of restructuring the world economy. The UN Charter and Universal Declaration of Human Rights have been adopted by all member states and embody some of the highest ideals expressed by humanity. If the UN is rendered more democratic and entrusted with more authority, it would be in a position to foster the growing sense of community between nations and harmonise global economic relationships.

Being human

Establishing more inclusive structures of global governance will only remedy one aspect of a complex system. Another key transformation that must take place is in our understanding and practice of 'economics' so that government policies can become closely aligned with urgent humanitarian and ecological needs.

The economic principles that have fashioned the world's existing global governance framework – particularly in relation to international trade and finance – can be traced back to the moral philosophy of Enlightenment thinkers during the emergence of industrial society in Britain. Drawing on the ideas of these early theorists, mainstream economists have assumed that human beings are inherently selfish, competitive, acquisitive and individualistic. Such notions about human nature are now firmly established as the principles upon which modern economies are built, and have been used to justify the proliferation of free markets as the best way to organise societies.

Particularly since the 1980s, these basic economic assumptions have increasingly dominated public policy and pushed aside ethical considerations in the pursuit of efficiency, short-term growth and profit maximisation. But the 'neoliberal' ideology that institutionalised greed and self-interest was fundamentally discredited by the collapse of banks and a world stock market crash in 2008. As a consequence, the global financial crisis reinvigorated a long-standing debate about the importance of morality and ethics in relation to the market economy.

At the same time, recent experiments by evolutionary biologists and neuro-cognitive scientists have demonstrated that human beings are biologically predisposed to cooperate and share. Without this evolutionary advantage, we may not have survived as a species. Anthropological findings have long supported this view of human nature, with case studies revealing that sharing and gifting often formed the basis of economic life in traditional societies, leading individuals to prioritise their social relationships above all other concerns. As a whole, these findings challenge many of the core assumptions of classical economic theory – in particular the firmly held belief that people in any society will always act competitively to maximise their economic interests.

If humanity is to survive the formidable challenges that define our generation – including climate change, diminishing fossil fuels and global conflict – it is necessary to forge new ethical understandings that embrace our collective values and global interdependence. We urgently need a new paradigm for human advancement, beginning with a fundamental reordering of world priorities: an immediate end to hunger, the securing of universal basic needs, and a rapid safeguarding of the environment and atmosphere. No longer can national self-interest, international competition and excessive commercialisation form the foundation of our global economic framework.

The crucial first step towards creating an inclusive world system requires overhauling our outdated assumptions about human nature, reconnecting our public life with fundamental values, and rethinking the role of markets in achieving the common good. In line with what we now know about human behaviour and psychology, integrating the principle of sharing into our economic system would reflect our global unity and have far-reaching implications for how we distribute and consume the planet's wealth and resources. Sharing the world's resources more equitably can allow us to build a more sustainable, cooperative and inclusive global economy – one that reflects and supports what it really means to be human.

This article has been adapted from sections of a recent booklet entitled *Sharing the World's Resources – An Introduction*. Rajesh Makwana is the director of Share The World's Resources and can be contacted at rajesh@stwr.org. Adam Parsons is the editor at Share The World's Resources and can be contacted at adam@stwr.org

17 January 2011

⇨ Information from Share The World's Resources. Visit www.stwr.org for more.

SHARE THE WORLD'S RESOURCES

Globalisation and the rise of the global middle class

Center for American progress partner in Britain examines rising living standards across the globe.

By Will Straw, Associate Director for Globalisation and Climate Change at the Institute for Public Policy Research

Analysis of globalisation in recent years has focused primarily on the 'supply shock' created by a huge increase in low-cost labour in China, India and other emerging markets. Citizens in the developed world view this as both positive, due to the falling cost of consumer goods, and negative, due to the perceived pressure on their jobs and wages.

But a new phase of globalisation is now under way due to the 'demand shock' caused by rising prosperity in

middle-income countries. Over the coming years, millions of people in the BRIC countries – Brazil, Russia, India and China – and elsewhere will be lifted out of poverty and see their disposable income rise. This creates challenges in resource scarcity and the impact on climate change while bringing great opportunities as businesses compete to meet the new demand for goods and services, and millions of jobs are created.

So how should developed countries respond? In March, Lord Peter Mandelson – who served in a number of cabinet positions under both Tony Blair and Gordon Brown – launched a major programme on the future of globalisation on behalf of the United Kingdom's leading progressive think tank, the Institute for Public Policy Research (IPPR). The research – which will conclude in January 2012 – looks at who benefits from globalisation, and examines what Lord Mandelson describes as 'two very different globalisations' defined as the 'Davos view of globalisation' seen from '10,000 feet' and the on-the-ground view where it seems that 'jobs and opportunities in the fast-developing world are created at the expense of our own employment and standard of living'.

Specifically, the research is examining four key questions:

⇨ How do domestic policy frameworks in developed countries – including industrial policy, fiscal policy, labour market regulation, skills and education and immigration – need to change to ensure both that developed economies can remain competitive and that trade delivers on progressive values at home?

⇨ How can Britain improve its export performance and plug its £27 billion export gap with the BRIC countries?

⇨ How can trade and open markets deliver maximum economic benefits for the world's poorest countries and help them deliver sustainable development for their people?

⇨ How do global and European economic institutions need to change to respond to the changing balance of economic and political power between regions and countries in order to deliver solutions to global economic challenges including trade liberalisation and global imbalances?

To help answer these questions, the research team is undertaking a series of fact-finding missions. So far we have visited two of the BRIC countries: Brazil and China.

In Brazil, we found an increasingly self-confident country that recently overtook Italy as the world's seventh-largest economy. Brazil's private sector is booming, having survived largely unscathed from the financial crisis. Meanwhile, the successful Bolsa Familia (family allowance) policy – which provides financial aid to poor families that enrol their children in elementary school – has helped reduce inequality, cut poverty levels and created 50 million consumers in the 'new middle class'.

Brazil's international economics policy is also dramatically shifting. Brazil is looking increasingly towards China and away from Europe, and business and government are both hardening their position towards further trade liberalisation. The upshot is that European countries will have to work harder to gain Brazil's attention. Lord Mandelson's review will examine ways in which European businesses should raise their profile in and increase their exports to Brazil.

In China, the recently published 12th five-year plan makes clear that China's development is 'unbalanced, uncoordinated and unsustainable' despite the economy's continued rapid growth. Key to addressing this is a rebalancing of China's economy towards domestic consumption, which currently stands at 35 per cent of GDP, and away from an overreliance on net exports and investment.

These themes are consistent with the Center for American Progress's 'virtuous circle' thesis, which outlined that raising Chinese demand through increased provision of social safety nets was critical to rebalancing the global economy.

Global businesses, including Hewlett Packard, which we visited in the rapidly growing city of Chongqing, are benefiting from this huge expansion in domestic Chinese demand for goods and services and the investment opportunities presented in China. The challenge in the years ahead is for China to open up more of its sectors to global competition and improve the ease of doing business in the country so smaller businesses and entrepreneurs can join multinationals in benefiting from these rapid changes. The IPPR review aims to set out how British and European firms can emulate the success of American firms like HP in benefiting from the increased Chinese demand.

Later this year, we will visit India, Germany, Belgium (seat of the European Union) and Washington, DC, to understand how other countries are coping with and thinking about the latest phase of globalisation. Decision-makers will need to consider policy implications at both the domestic and international level.

Our leaders need to consider:

⇨ How we provide industrial support for key sectors where competitive advantage lies.

⇨ How we continue to raise the education and skill levels of our workforce to ensure that businesses have the people they need.

⇨ How to reform our labour market policies to ensure that those in work are properly rewarded for their endeavours and that those who miss out or find themselves unemployed are given support and treated with dignity as they get back into the labour market.

Internationally, we will need to work much more closely with other countries to ensure that global solutions can be found to a range of issues from creating a level playing field for companies competing in the global economy to mitigating the impact of climate change to preventing another financial crash decimating much of the world's productive capacity.

None of this is easy, but a unilateral approach that seeks to ignore these trends is not the answer. Countries such as Britain and the United States must engage multilaterally to ensure that the global economy works better for their citizens and that the next set of global rules enhance rather than diminish that shared prosperity.

Views expressed are those of the author and do not necessarily reflect the position of the Center for American Progress. The authors and institutions that produced this material are a part of the Just Jobs Network.

30 August 2011

⇨ Information from the Center for American Progress. Visit www.americanprogress.org for more.

© *Center for American Progress*

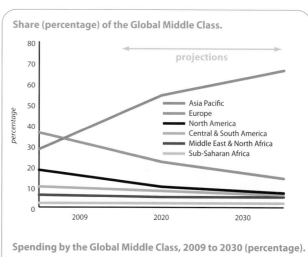

Source: The Emerging Middle Class in Developing Countries, Kharas, H., 2010, tables 2 and 3. OECD Development Centre, January 2010.

CENTER FOR AMERICAN PROGRESS

Globalisation can work, but only with a unified international plan

We desperately need economic and social institutions working across national borders.

By Will Hutton

Britain has become a hub in the global web of car and engine production. This year, 1.4 million cars and more than three million engines will be produced here, most of them for export. The research-and-development spend in the industry is high and rising, while Tata's purchase of Jaguar Land Rover has proved one of its best-ever investments, as it now produces nearly three-quarters of the company's total profits. All considered, this is a modern capitalist success story and if and when the economy rebalances, production of this type will grow even further.

However, all this success is accompanied by very few new jobs. Fewer than 150,000 jobs are directly involved in the making of all those cars and engines and the numbers have been gently falling for years as modern production techniques transform productivity. Tata is building a new engine plant in Wolverhampton that will be a world leader in low-carbon engines; it might create 750 jobs.

Meanwhile, McDonald's has announced that it will be creating another 2,500 jobs this year. Hamburger flipping creates jobs and these jobs do require more than a modicum of skill and capacity to handle often truculent customers. But McJobs are never likely to be highly paid, high-value-added jobs. Nor will McDonald's earn Britain much in the way of export revenue.

There's a similar pattern across the industrialised West, raising anxious and urgent questions about whether the modern economy can create mass employment at worthwhile wages. Yes, there is a manufacturing core that puts production on sites across the globe but that creates few jobs in a country such as Britain. And there is a modest service sector, which is either integrated with the manufacturers or, as is the case with fast food, which provides self-standing services in its own right. Beyond these, there's a vast web of 'cream-skimming' services associated with brokerage and agency – everything from investment banking to headhunters, estate agents and football agents – taking a cut on some transaction or deal but adding precious little value despite sky-high personal rewards. Let's call this 'agentist' capitalism.

At a dinner with Apple's Steve Jobs, President Obama asked him if the US's most successful and profitable company would ever bring some of the work it is generating back to the US. Never, replied Jobs. Apple, like Britain's car industry, is embedded in its global production networks.

Without globalisation, this new economic structure and accompanying pattern of reward would be impossible. But there is another twist: this 'enabling' globalisation is itself unstable. It rests on countries such as Germany, China, India and Japan – which do most of the producing in the new global supply chains – building up never-ending trade surpluses, while other countries carry deficits, with no mechanism compelling either side to change. The banking system is then obliged to recycle the surpluses, exploiting the many loopholes to create an unregulated shadow system, which has now imploded.

George Osborne writes in the *Financial Times* that we are living through less a crisis of capitalism than a crisis

The global production network...

Britain — Burger flipper

USA — Company CEO

China — Electronics assembler

Greece — Small businesswoman

in confidence, without ever inquiring whether those who have lost confidence might have some very good reasons for doing so. Lord Mandelson, once no less an innocent cheerleader for markets and globalisation, last week issued an extraordinary recantation. He told the BBC's *Today* programme that he would never now, as he did in 1998, say he was intensely relaxed about businessmen becoming filthy rich doing whatever they chose.

Moreover, as he introduced *Making the third wave of globalisation work for us all*, a new report by the centre-left think tank IPPR, Mandelson urged a strengthening in global governance along with a serious commitment at home to industrial policy, a robust social safety net and regulation of errant business. Otherwise, he warned, the legitimacy of globalisation and modern capitalism would become profoundly questioned. Enlightened self-interest must prompt governments and business into a major change of direction.

Without globalisation, this new economic structure and accompanying pattern of reward would be impossible. But there is another twist: this 'enabling' globalisation is itself unstable

---

It is an important intervention and Mandelson has unexpected allies at the IMF and World Bank. But the debate has to go further still. The decline of productive, high-employment capitalism is most marked in the English-speaking countries of the 'Anglosphere' – the countries most committed to the notion that markets are brilliantly wise and never need challenging.

These are the economies where 'agentism' has gone furthest, the productive sector has shrunk most and where the resulting inequalities of income and opportunity have become most acute. All economies have their agentist service sector, but in the UK and US it has become over-large and over-rewarded. There has been an indifference, especially in the UK, to building the ecosystem that delivers productive enterprise. Instead, the doctrine, even if it is now changing somewhat, and erratically, has been to do the opposite. The consequent 'squeezed middle' and doubts about modern capitalism are as much doubts about agentism as they are about globalisation.

There are multiple threats to confront. Only so much can be expected from enlightened self-interest. We need some counterbalancing international forces to hold government, business and banks to account. What is striking, for example, in the protests in Greece, Portugal and Ireland against the austerity packages is that they are so firmly national. There has not been

one high-profile joint press conference, for example, of those parties in all three countries that oppose the measures. Not even the protesters or the trade unions make common cause. Nor has there been any practical prospectus for what could and should be different.

British trade unions are often attacked for being intellectually moribund and permanently on the defensive. But these are weaknesses they share with their counterparts elsewhere. The Occupy movement is a beginning, but it is transient. If the world is to have a constructive counterbalance to globalisation, then it needs grounded social institutions that work across borders and are likely to endure.

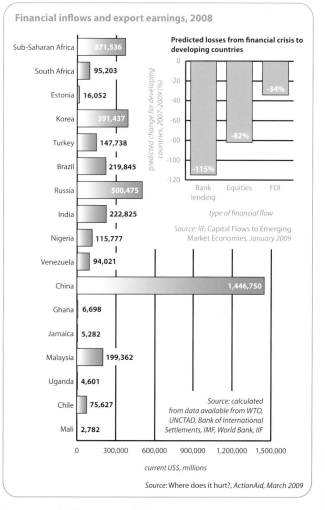

Financial inflows and export earnings, 2008

Predicted losses from financial crisis to developing countries

Source: IIF, Capital Flows to Emerging Market Economies, January 2009

	current US$, millions
Sub-Saharan Africa	371,536
South Africa	95,203
Estonia	16,052
Korea	391,437
Turkey	147,738
Brazil	219,845
Russia	500,475
India	222,825
Nigeria	115,777
Venezuela	94,021
China	1,446,750
Ghana	6,698
Jamaica	5,282
Malaysia	199,362
Uganda	4,601
Chile	75,627
Mali	2,782

Source: calculated from data available from WTO, UNCTAD, Bank of International Settlements, IMF, World Bank, IIF

Source: Where does it hurt?, ActionAid, March 2009

One would be powerful transnational trade unions, committed not to socialising the global means of production, but to insisting on worldwide responsible capitalism – and creating new levers to get it. A pipedream? Something has to change. We can retreat to our national *laagers*, which would be an economic disaster, or we can build an interdependent world that works. There is only one option to choose.

⇨ This article first appeared in *The Observer*, 29 January 2012

THE OBSERVER

Globalisation has turned on its Western creators

From the Occupy Wall Street and Tea Party movements of the US to the rise of populist politics in Europe, the globalisation backlash is everywhere.

By Jeremy Warner

A number of years ago, a story went around that sprouts were being transported from across Britain to an East Anglian airport, from where they were sent to Poland for washing and packaging before being air-freighted back again for sale in supermarkets located but a few miles from where they were grown.

This is an extreme example of the sometimes insane supply-chain dynamics of modern-day globalisation, but it speaks loudly to widespread disillusionment with the once-unquestioned blessings of free trade. From the Occupy Wall Street and Tea Party movements of the US to the renewed rise of populist politics in Europe, the backlash is everywhere to be seen.

> *By opening up the global economy to Asia, Latin America and Eastern Europe, the West seems to have unleashed a doomsday machine which threatens ever-greater destruction of its own living standards*

In real terms, Americans are on average no better off than they were 30 years ago; in Britain, the Institute for Fiscal Studies says that our real disposable incomes are in the midst of a 14-year freeze. Vast tracts of gainful employment in textiles, potteries, shoe-making, machine tools and many other industries have disappeared, to be replaced by... well, not very much at all outside the now languishing financial services industry and the housing market.

The West's competitive advantage, even in hi-tech industries such as pharmaceuticals and aerospace, is being fast whittled away too. The welfare and health entitlements to which we have become accustomed look ever more unaffordable, while the final-salary pensions that workers could once expect as reward for a lifetime of service are now confined to the public sector – and those too will surely be gone within ten years. It is small wonder that the benefits of free trade are now so widely questioned.

Critics of globalisation, such as Joseph Stiglitz, the Nobel laureate in economics, used to focus on the supposed harm that Western-inspired trade liberalisation was inflicting on the developing world. Few would these days think this the correct way of looking at the problem.

On the contrary, by opening up the global economy to Asia, Latin America and Eastern Europe, the West seems to have unleashed a doomsday machine which threatens ever-greater destruction of its own living standards. After a brief number of years in which globalisation made everything seemingly cheaper, the terms of trade have moved badly against the West.

Sure enough, the world as a whole is getting a whole lot richer. In the past decade alone, the global economy has doubled in size. But most of the benefits of this explosion in activity have gone to the developing world and, in the West, the already rich, highly educated and talented. The wealth divide has widened to record levels almost everywhere.

Western business leaders embraced globalisation not just because it opens up new markets, introduces new ideas and weeds out unproductive, protected sectors, but because it allows for lower production costs and so bigger profits. It doesn't seem to have occurred to them that if you don't provide Western consumers with jobs, they'll be priced out of the market and the mother economy will wither and die.

> *Western business leaders embraced globalisation not just because it opens up new markets, introduces new ideas and weeds out unproductive, protected sectors, but because it allows for lower production costs and so bigger profits*

The principles of free trade are the same for nations as they are for individuals. Rather than trying to produce everything we need to live, most of us choose to work in quite specialist forms of employment, the product of which we sell to others. We then use the proceeds to buy in other goods and services. Nations ought similarly to derive a collective economic benefit by specialising in the things they do best and then trading with others for the rest.

But the system only works if everyone plays by a common set of rules and standards. Nations won't live happily together if they don't. That's what has gone wrong with globalisation. Many have just copied from the West and used cheap labour for competitive advantage. Adam Smith's 'invisible hand' cannot operate efficiently in a world of wildly different labour standards, attitudes to the rule of law and manipulated currency values. Even Smith, the father of free market thinking, recognised that markets must be policed if they are to function properly.

The Chinese are not going to get serious about intellectual property rights until they are inventing more things than they steal, nor are they going to engage in worthwhile currency reform until they have spirited every last job possible from the once vibrant West. It might be argued, as it sometimes is by Chinese officials, that they are levelling the playing field after several hundred years of relative deprivation. That's surely the way it is meant to work, with pursuit of self-interest working for the greatest common good. The West thought it could benefit from globalisation; it ill becomes advanced economies to complain now that they are losing from it.

All the same, the world needs urgently to embrace new forms of multi-lateralism and cooperation if it is not to slip back into an age of protectionist infighting. The free market system has become distorted to the point of virtual collapse. Unsustainable trade imbalances are the major underlying cause of today's rolling series of debt crises in advanced economies.

In the long run, all nations must become better balanced and self-reliant. It was madness to outsource so much of what we used to do to foreign climes, just as it is unsustainable for China and other surplus nations to rely on ever-growing exports.

Where are the jobs going to come from, it is often despairingly asked, in Western economies? There's a simple, if challenging answer: by returning to the way we were and doing more things locally. And that starts with washing our own sprouts for the Christmas dinner table.

7 December 2011

Trade

Information from CAFOD.

What is trade?

When you buy a computer game or a bar of chocolate, you are 'trading': exchanging money for goods. Workers, companies, countries and consumers take part in trade. Workers make or grow the goods. Companies pay the workers and sell what they produce. Governments encourage companies to set up; they create jobs, generate taxes and earn foreign currency. Consumers buy the end product.

Who sells what?

Some developing countries, particularly in Asia, are major manufacturing powers; others, mainly African countries, sell commodities, like coffee, cocoa and cotton, and raw materials like copper. For most it's a mix; Brazil sells aircraft but is still the world's largest coffee producer. In developing countries costs are lower, especially wages, so their factories can make goods more cheaply.

Raw materials

Countries that produce only raw materials and commodities are at a disadvantage.

⇨ They don't gain from processing: for example, if countries which export cocoa beans made chocolate, more of the final price for chocolate paid by consumers in the UK would stay in the country of origin.

⇨ The price of raw materials and commodities often change, making it hard to plan.

Try this

Look at the labels in your clothes. Decide why you think the clothes were made in these countries.

Choose a product and draw a diagram of how you think trade works for this product.

Fact

US retail giant Wal-Mart employs more than two million people worldwide (UNCTAD 2008). The ranking list of top multinational companies in the world includes: Vodafone, Ford, Nestlé, Wal-Mart, Sony, and Procter and Gamble.

Try this

Guess the names of five other top 40 companies. Check if you are right by going to unctad.org and looking at the table on 'The world's top 100 non-financial TNCs, ranked by foreign assets'. Find the home country of the top ten companies.

Fact

In 2008 Fairtrade chocolate made up less than one per cent of the market in the UK. By the end of 2010, it made up around ten per cent and reached the milestone of £1 billion in sales.

⇨ Prices for raw materials and commodities are often very low.

Manufactured goods

Factories and other industries mean jobs, but there are downsides too:

⇨ It can be hard for some countries to move on to making more valuable manufactured goods like cars. They may have the raw materials, but may not have the technology or the infrastructure. Established manufacturers in other countries have a huge lead.

⇨ Jobs may not be secure. Competition is fierce and companies will fail if they cannot produce the quality and price that international buyers want.

⇨ Producing the best product at the cheapest prices can mean cutting corners on health and safety, paying low wages and pressurising people to work long hours.

'We cannot proceed to increase the wealth and power of the rich while we entrench the needy in their poverty and add to the woes of the oppressed.' Pope Paul VI

Tariffs

Tariffs are taxes on imported goods. High tariffs can be used to protect domestic producers from foreign competition. Developing countries want the freedom to raise tariffs because their industries cannot compete with established manufacturers in more advanced countries. Trade rules prevent them from doing this. The UK and other rich countries preach free trade, that is, a world of low tariffs, but when the UK was building up its own industries in the 19th century, it protected them from foreign competition. It's a case of 'Do as we say', not 'Do as we did'.

CAFOD

Tariffs on manufactured goods imported into rich countries are generally very low[1] but are much higher for agricultural imports.[2] This hurts the poorest countries, where more than half the population works in agriculture. Some allowances have been made for the very poorest countries but the global economic crisis is making any benefits more difficult to achieve. Poor countries have suffered more from a decline in exports than rich (*Millennium Development Report* 2010).

There are also non-tariff barriers, for example quality and food safety controls which are very strict, setting standards which are often difficult for producers in developing countries to achieve.

Trade rules

The World Trade Organization (WTO) sets the trade rules, but still uses rules negotiated in 1994 which allow rich countries to support or subsidise their farmers. This means that farmers often produce more than they can sell in their own country. The surplus may be sent to poor countries and sold there at an artificially low price that local people cannot match. Poor countries want to be allowed to raise tariffs to keep out cheap imported food that threaten their farmers' livelihoods. But rich countries won't agree.

Although China, India and other large developing countries, known as 'emerging economies', have now become major trading powers, the poorest countries are still at a disadvantage. They can't afford expert delegations at the WTO so cannot participate effectively in negotiations which could affect them.

Case study – cotton crisis

Benin, Burkino Faso, Chad and Mali are able to produce the cheapest cotton in the world. Exports should be propelling ten million African farmers out of poverty. But subsidies to US cotton farmers mean that West African farmers can't make any money from exporting their cotton because they can't compete with the artificially cheap price. Production in Africa has halved since 2005.

The power of multinationals

World trade is dominated by 80,000 multinational corporations (MNCs), large companies with a presence in many parts of the world. MNCs account for 70 per cent of world trade. The top 100 MNCs employ over 15 million people. MNCs employ lawyers and lobbyists to influence governments as they negotiate for trade rules favourable to them.

Governments keen to benefit from international trade encourage foreign companies to invest in their countries. However, factories producing goods for sale in rich countries, especially garment factories, are increasingly owned by developing country firms. Huge companies like Nike and Marks and Spencer do not own the factories producing their goods, but local companies make the products to their specification. If the factory fails to reach the required standard, the company can always find one that will.

The future

CAFOD and many other organisations campaign for trade justice – for development issues to be taken into consideration in trade agreements. Trade justice would guarantee higher, more stable prices for producers in developing countries. Meanwhile, voluntary schemes can make a difference:

⇨ The Fairtrade Foundation, which CAFOD helped to create, works with producers in developing countries, guaranteeing them a fair price. This means that the price paid will always cover the costs of production, however low the international price. The Fairtrade label identifies goods belonging to this scheme.

⇨ The Ethical Trading Initiative (ETI) sets minimum standards on wages and working conditions. Companies buying manufactured goods from developing countries work with the ETI to try and ensure that the workers are treated fairly and paid properly.

Useful websites

Fairtrade Foundation: fairtrade.org.uk

World Trade Organization: wto.org

Ethical Trading Initiative: www.eti.org.uk

UN Millennium Development Goals: un.org/millennium goals

Trade Justice Movement (a coalition of 60 organisations, including CAFOD): tjm.org.uk

'Trading Visions' focuses on the voices of small-scale producers in developing countries: tradingvisions.org

Notes

1   1.51% for the European Union and 3.03% for the United States (see nationsencyclopedia.com/WorldStats/UNCTAD-importrates-manufactured-goods.html)

2   18% in the European Union (2007) – (*International Herald Tribune* 26 Feb 2007)

All facts correct May 2011

⇨ The above information is reprinted with kind permission from CAFOD. Visit their website at www.cafod.org.uk for more information on this and other related topics.

© CAFOD

CAFOD

Trade and economic growth

Information from the Department for International Development.

Expanding markets and trade

Trade is the lifeblood of global economies. Trade is a stimulus for growth and productivity, and allows a country to expand its horizons beyond its national boundaries. Trade has a direct impact on poverty: on average, an increase in trade volumes of 10% will raise incomes by 5%. Countries which miss out on the benefits of global trade are locked out of opportunities to profit from international expertise, low-cost production inputs and much-needed technology.

The opportunities to improve the lives of poor people through trade are huge: in Vietnam, export-led growth rates of 7–8% reduced poverty rates from 58% in 1993 to 16% in 2006. There are many prospects to open up global and regional trade further to benefit developing countries. At present, Africa accounts for just 3% of global trade. African countries trade, on average, just 10% of their goods with each other, compared to 65% between European countries.

Reducing the costs of trading

The UK is committed to reducing the costs and time taken to trade in developing countries by collaboration with governments and economic communities. DFID's new African Free Trade Initiative will support integration and provide technical expertise to unlock issues that continue to hold back economic growth across the region.

Our Regional East Africa Integration and TradeMark East Africa programmes aim to achieve a 5–10% reduction in the average trade transport costs in East Africa through better border management, and agree common procedures across East African countries for transport and logistics.

In Chirundu, a border between Zambia and Zimbabwe, DFID supported the creation of a 'one-stop border post' to streamline customs procedures and cut red tape. It will take an anticipated three hours instead of three days to cross the border. In Sierra Leone, DFID support is helping to automate customs clearing procedures to reduce waiting times from six days to two days by 2012.

Opening markets

The Government's recent White Paper *Trade and Investment for Growth* marked a redoubling of DFID's efforts to open global market opportunities to developing countries. We will press for EU preference schemes and trade agreements to be reformed in ways that enhance opportunities for trade for developing countries. The UK will continue to lobby within the G20 countries to provide 100% Duty Free Quota Free Market Access for Least Developed Countries, estimated to be worth up to $7 billion a year for their exports.

> *The UK is committed to reducing the costs and time taken to trade in developing countries by collaboration with governments and economic communities*

Raising the bar on working conditions

DFID is committed to improving working conditions for people in developing countries, often working in international supply chains. We provide backing to both the Ethical Trading Initiative (ETI), which drives better working conditions for 8.6 million workers in 40,000 supplier companies, and Fairtrade International which ensures that farmers receive fair prices for their products and workers receive better wages. DFID has established the Responsible and Accountable Garment Sector Challenge Fund which is working in Bangladesh, India, Nepal and Lesotho to stimulate and encourage better working conditions, particularly for female workers, in export garment factories.

Creating and sustaining market linkages

It is challenging for smallholder farmers to access overseas markets because of the relatively small quantities produced and the demanding quality standards required. In Mozambique, exports of fish are an important source of income. DFID is helping the industry to maintain its EU standards accreditation, thereby safeguarding 70,000 jobs.

⇨ The above information is reprinted with kind permission from the Department for International Development. Visit www.dfid.gov.uk for more information.

© Crown copyright

Questions and answers on trade

Information from ActionAid.

What do you mean by global trade?

Trade is something people and companies do every day – the buying and selling of goods and services. People have traded for centuries in order to overcome local scarcities. It can involve local transactions, such as food from a farmers' market or purchasing a hair cut. Today trade is far more global, made easier by efficient modes of transport and communications. Fresh fruits and vegetables can be supplied and bought from countries such as South Africa and New Zealand and services such as call centres are now supplied from almost anywhere in the world.

Many governments intervene in the trading system to support local firms and farmers and to protect the environment (commonly known as protectionism). Alternatively, many governments have decided to open up their trading markets (commonly known as 'free trade' or trade liberalisation) in the belief that more trade between nations will stimulate growth and ultimately increase prosperity.

What is wrong with global trade?

Although trade has the potential to lift millions of people out of poverty, poor countries are getting a raw deal under the current global trading system. Trade is overseen at a global level by the World Trade Organization (WTO), which believes in free trade, as do global institutions such as the International Monetary Fund (IMF) and the World Bank.

Rich countries, particularly the US and those in the EU, are trying to force poor countries to open their markets to goods and services from big business, threatening the livelihoods of hundreds of thousands of farmers and forcing local companies out of business.

What's the evidence?

Because trade has far-reaching effects, often outside people's control, the free trade policies pushed by rich countries are failing to bring prosperity to those who need it most. The poorest countries have actually become poorer over the past two decades, with 80% of their populations now living on $2 a day or less (and half living on $1 a day). The gap between the rich and the poor is expanding.

In Ghana, two million people living in the Northern and Upper West regions depend on farming as a way of life and a means of survival. Food crops like tomatoes, rice, okra and onions are grown, accounting for 90 per cent of employment and income. However, the relaxing of import tariffs in the 1990s saw cheap rice flood into the country as well as heavily subsidised rice from the EU.

The effect on local communities was disastrous. John Ayariga, a rice farmer from Bolgatanga in the Upper East region, explains: 'I have been a farmer for 19 years. I started farming at age 12. Rice farming is no longer lucrative because imported rice is cheaper than locally produced rice. We cannot make ends meet. The field we used to plant rice in is now lying fallow and is being used to play football. Is this fair? There's no pride in being a farmer now.'

What is the difference between free trade and Trade Justice?

Free trade and 'Trade Justice' are opposite sides of the same coin. Perfect free trade means removing all barriers to trade between countries. All too often, this means putting the pursuit of free trade above other objectives such as reducing poverty, protecting the environment and people's rights. Free trade includes removing all forms of government support to farmers, slashing farm tariffs and removing quotas on goods coming into a country. No country has ever gone to this extreme but 'free trade policies' are those which move a country in this direction.

Trade Justice allows developing country governments to freely choose the best policies without being limited by the WTO and other global institutions such as the World Bank and IMF. Governments would be able to intervene in their national economies to protect their farmers and developing industries. Trade Justice means that rich countries would stop harmful practices such as paying massive subsidies to their farmers and dumping farm goods in poor countries, and would properly regulate big business.

No country has ever become a 'developed country' by pursuing free trade policies from the outset. Rich countries have used the 'Trade Justice' approach to get where they are today – but are now denying the same chance to poor countries.

Isn't free trade the way out of poverty?

Rich countries say free trade is the best way out of poverty for developing countries. However, free trade forces rich and poor to compete on equal terms. In such an unequal world, this kind of trade would be far from fair. It would be like pitching Manchester United against the village football team – there might be a level playing field, but Manchester United will still win every time.

There is very little evidence to support claims that free trade lifts people out of poverty – in fact, the opposite is true. Countries that have rapidly opened their markets to free trade, such as Haiti, Nepal, Mali, Zambia and Peru, have very poor records on economic growth and poverty reduction. On the other hand, countries such and Taiwan and South Korea opted to protect their domestic industries rather than completely open their economies to global trade. As a result, this not only produced higher economic growth but also resulted in lower inequality in both countries.

In recent years, India – where 80% of people live in extreme poverty – has reduced its import taxes on industrial goods such as textiles and leather. This has resulted in a massive increase of imported industrial goods and has left many of the 30 million people employed in the textiles sector out of work and destitute, especially women. Vishambar, a 35-year-old silk weaver from Varanasi, is one of those who lost their jobs. 'There is no work,' he says. 'I am just sitting begging…I want work for myself and for other people in the village.'

Although rich countries push for freer trade, no country has ever developed by following a free-trade model from the outset.

Yet the world's richest countries continue to force the poorest to open their markets to unfair competition – allowing big business to reap the benefits. This has led to a 'race to the bottom', damaging workers' rights and contributing to environmental devastation. Almost all rich countries developed by selectively protecting and supporting their own economies. Now they are on top, they are kicking away the ladder for developing countries.

What about Fairtrade products?

Fairtrade refers to a system which allows farmers in developing countries to get a fair price for the goods they sell abroad. Fairtrade consists of a very specific range of products available to Western consumers. Fairtrade goods have been certified by the Fairtrade Foundation (a charity). Farmers are paid a higher price than the current global price for their goods and have certain rights, such as being able to join a trade union.

Western consumers pay more for fairtrade tea, coffee, chocolate, etc. to ensure that producers in developing countries get a better deal.

If everyone bought Fairtrade products, wouldn't that solve the problem?

No. The number of Fairtrade products is still relatively small. Unless you're going to drink coffee and eat chocolate all day it's likely you'll have to consume goods that aren't Fairtrade! Fairtrade primarily helps those who sell their goods abroad. The very poorest farmers produce for local consumers, not foreign ones. They are being pushed out of those markets by goods sold cheaply below the cost of production by big corporations based in rich countries and then dumped into developing countries' markets. Although this system benefits some farmers in developing countries, Fairtrade products represent less than 1% of global trade. So while Fairtrade helps, it's only 'trade justice' that will begin to solve the wider problem of unfair trade.

⇨ Information from ActionAid: taken from their website. Visit www.actionaid.org.uk for more.

Trade glossary

Developing world

A collective term used to describe the world's developing countries: countries where average income is very low and most of the population is considered very poor. Other terms used include low-income countries, majority world, the South or the Third World.

Dumping

When a country or countries sell their unwanted surplus produce at a price below the cost of producing it. This is unfair to farmers in the countries which buy it.

Exports

To sell goods or services to a buyer outside your country.

Imports

Goods and services that one country buys from other countries.

Subsidy, subsidised, subsidising

A subsidy is a payment, generally by a government, to a producer, e.g. a farmer, to encourage its production. This in effect makes the product cheaper to grow or produce and it can therefore be sold more cheaply to buyers and consumers. This means that in many poor countries it becomes cheaper to buy imported food than to buy it from local farmers. This in turn puts local farmers out of business.

Livelihoods

The way that people make their living and have reliable and permanent sources of food, income, and employment. Trade has a big impact on people's livelihoods. Over two-thirds of the three billion people living in poverty rely on small-scale agriculture for their food and wages. Trade rules and subsidies which benefit rich countries destroy the livelihoods of the poor.

Tariff

A tax placed on an imported good or service.

Quota

A limit to the number of imports of a particular kind that a country will accept.

Markets, poverty and Fair Trade

Information from the Adam Smith Institute.

By Sam Bowman

I was at the Burgess Hill Fair Trade Festival on Wednesday, debating whether Fair Trade was a help or a hindrance to the developing world. I must have surprised them by being quite ambivalent about the topic: I was supposed to be arguing against it, but I had some quite positive things to say about Fair Trade. What I really wanted to argue was that our trade structures have to change if we're serious about fighting poverty on a respectable scale.

People have a tendency to pitch Fair Trade against free trade, as if there's a tension between the two. Quite the opposite, really – Fair Trade is quite a good example of how consumers in a free market can use their buying power to effect change that they want. I think a lot of people on the free market side have (unfairly) seen Fair Trade as being anti-market, but I see no difference between paying for the satisfaction of giving money to a Fair Trade farmer, and paying for the satisfaction of driving a nicer car. It's part of the market mechanism, and a very nice example of how individuals' purchasing power can advance the social goals that they like. And it makes a nice change from the people who want the Government to sort out the world's problems.

Nevertheless, Fair Trade is still a flawed system. Most Fair Trade farmers are in Latin America, even though poverty is generally far worse in Africa – so buying Fair Trade coffee over non-Fair Trade coffee can mean that your money goes to a Mexican rather than a Kenyan farmer. This may change, but right now the fact is that Fair Trade products can deprive the world's poorest farmers of their income in favour of relatively well-off ones. And if it gets bigger, Fair Trade risks affecting global supply and disincentivising other types of production in the developing world. This probably isn't a problem right now, because Fair Trade is a very small part of the market, but someday it might be.

There are also lots of alternatives to Fair Trade – in an excellent IEA report on the topic, Sushil Mohan points out that gourmet coffee growers in Rwanda have been able to achieve prices as high as $55/kilo, versus the market average of $1.30/kilo for ordinary-grade beans. To be fair to my debate opponent, he didn't claim that Fair Trade was perfect.

The most important point to remember when thinking about Fair Trade is that, while it's a decent humanitarian mechanism, it won't do much to help poor countries' economic growth. For that, they need to be able to trade freely with us. The EU's monstrous Common Agricultural Policy simultaneously subsidises European farmers with one hand, and imposes extortionate tariffs on goods from the developing world with the other. The one comparative advantage that poor countries might have is thus nullified at taxpayers' expense.

I'm relaxed about Fair Trade, and I admire its supporters' use of exchange-based market mechanisms to advance their goals. There's no contradiction between Fair Trade and free trade – but achieving the latter is a lot more important.

11 March 2011

⇨ The above information is reprinted with kind permission from the Adam Smith Institute. Visit www.adamsmith.org for more information.

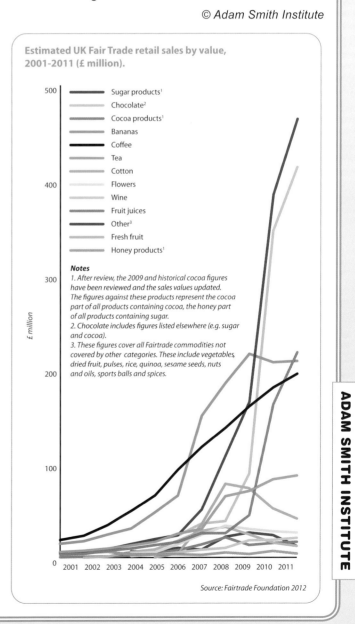

Estimated UK Fair Trade retail sales by value, 2001-2011 (£ million).

- Sugar products[1]
- Chocolate[2]
- Cocoa products[1]
- Bananas
- Coffee
- Tea
- Cotton
- Flowers
- Wine
- Fruit juices
- Other[3]
- Fresh fruit
- Honey products[1]

Notes
1. After review, the 2009 and historical cocoa figures have been reviewed and the sales values updated. The figures against these products represent the cocoa part of all products containing cocoa, the honey part of all products containing sugar.
2. Chocolate includes figures listed elsewhere (e.g. sugar and cocoa).
3. These figures cover all Fairtrade commodities not covered by other categories. These include vegetables, dried fruit, pulses, rice, quinoa, sesame seeds, nuts and oils, sports balls and spices.

Source: Fairtrade Foundation 2012

ADAM SMITH INSTITUTE

Put your best foot forward: the theory of free trade

Information from Global Footprints.

Some countries are 'better' at producing certain types of product than others. They can produce the goods or services more cheaply, quickly or efficiently. They have workers with particular skills or they have the land, climate and resources that other countries lack. As a simple example, the UK does not have a climate suitable for growing bananas, and therefore needs to import these from a country which has the right conditions for growing them.

It seems to make sense, then, for countries to specialise in producing the goods and services that they are best at and to trade these for things they are less good at producing or cannot produce at all. This is known as the principle of free trade.

Free trade trampling on the poor

With each country specialising in what they are best at producing and selling, free trade should benefit all countries. But in fact, free trade has resulted in very unequal trade. The 48 poorest countries, home to ten per cent of the world's population, have seen their share of exports decline to less than half a per cent of the world total in the last 20 years. The US and European countries, on the other hand, containing roughly the same number of people, account for nearly 50 per cent of world exports.

One of the reasons for this massive imbalance is the fact that the richer and more powerful countries grant subsidies to their own producers and protect themselves against cheaper imports by imposing tariffs and quotas. They also dump surplus produce on poorer countries, often at prices lower than it would cost farmers there to produce them.

In theory, there is an organisation which should prevent poor countries being trampled on. The World Trade Organization (WTO), which has 150 member nations, makes and enforces rules about international trade. The WTO is meant to help trade flow smoothly by solving disagreements about trade between different countries. However, critics of the WTO say that the rich countries have too much influence in the WTO and create rules of trade that are unfair on poorer countries. They also say the organisation has too much power compared with other international organisations. The decisions that it makes often take priority over agreements on the environment and international law, for example.

Did you know?

There are powerful people walking the corridors of the WTO...

Powerful WTO members stand accused of bullying weaker ones into agreeing to unfair trade rules. The US has been known to threaten to withdraw aid to countries if they do not support what the US wants in terms of trade rules. And while each member country in theory has an equal vote, in practice a lot depends on the number of delegates countries can afford to send. For example, at the WTO summit in Hong Kong in 2005, European countries had a record-breaking 832 delegates, the US 356, Japan 229. Meanwhile, 46 of the poorest countries had fewer than ten delegates.

Free trade trampling on the environment

Free trade can also be harmful to the environment. In the past, our fresh food was produced by local farmers. This was because fresh food is perishable and it could not be transported long distances without going off. But today, the transport of food by air, together with new methods of harvesting, storage and refrigeration, means that the food sold in our shops comes from all over the world. The energy involved and carbon dioxide emitted in flying food all over the world means we have increased our trade footprint dramatically.

Also, free trade rules imposed by the World Trade Organization make it increasingly difficult for small traders in poor countries to compete with large rich multinational companies, particularly when these companies are able to benefit from subsidies.

Did you know?

Some countries have experienced dumping, where farmers from rich countries flood their markets with cheap imports such as rice, tomatoes and chickens, pushing prices even lower. An example is Ghana. When the Government passed laws to protect its local rice growers from subsidised imports, the IMF forced it to tear up the law; now the US provides 40% of Ghana's rice, which has destroyed many local farmers' livelihoods.

⇨ The above information is reprinted with kind permission from HEC Global Learning Centre and the Global Footprints website. Visit www.globalfootprints.org for more.

Globalisation, UK poverty and communities

The implications of globalisation for poverty and communities in the UK – conclusion.

Globalisation affects many aspects of everyday life for people in the UK. It opens up opportunities for rapid contact between people around the world and increases the choices for some in work and in life as a whole. However, the increasing connections between people and global processes have not always been a positive experience for everyone. Globalisation has significantly different consequences for communities and households in the UK. This raises implications for policy, practice and research in a number of areas.

The global economy and experiences of work in the UK

The Joseph Rowntree Foundation programme found that some people experienced a heightened sense of anxiety about the security of their work and future employment opportunities for their children. They felt their working conditions had worsened with the increased use of contract and agency workers, and competition from migrant workers employed at lower salaries, sometimes overriding collective agreements. The financial crisis has exacerbated this.

The introduction of the EU Agency Workers Directive into the UK on 1 October 2011 should help address some of the employment issues raised by research participants, to ensure more equal treatment of agency and permanent workers. Close monitoring of how it is applied will be important, as will ensuring that people are aware of its contents and their rights under it.

This JRF research programme raises the broader question of what policies and practices best promote a combination of decent work, economic security and positive social outcomes in an open economy. JRF work on future labour markets is looking at some aspects of this key issue (www.jrf.org.uk/work/workarea/future-labour-markets). Discussion is also taking place in various policy circles, such as via the EU Employment and Growth Open Method of Coordination and peer review processes. However, future policy development in the UK may benefit from a debate involving a broader range of participants involved in economic and social policy about the approaches and experiences of different countries in managing an open economy while also tackling poverty and disadvantage.

The global economic crisis

People on low incomes in the UK have faced further hardship during the global economic crisis, as patterns of rising global food and fuel costs have been reflected in an increased cost of living at household level. Job losses and reduced hours have resulted in sudden changes in

household income as local employment has also suffered. The research showed that people on low incomes are facing considerable hardship in these conditions, often experiencing additional hidden time and other costs in their efforts to cope. It emphasised the importance of flexible welfare support and also support from family, friends and local groups to enable people to cope. Close monitoring of the implementation and impact of the Government's proposed Universal Credit will be important to ensure that it makes welfare support flexible. Support to local groups who play a valuable role – but not without cost to them – in helping people cope is also important for them to be able to sustain their role in helping build local resilience to an economic crisis that has its roots in global processes.

Global influences on the cost of living for people on low incomes

Initial research suggests that global influences are having an impact on the cost of living for people on low incomes, which is rising faster than standard inflation indices. Further analysis is needed to explore the relationships in more detail, but the potential impact over the next ten years may be significant. More consideration is also needed of the range of options open to the UK to ensure that globalisation does not result in price trends which exclude people on low incomes from affording at least a minimum standard of living. Options include measures to influence prices, although these may be limited. Interventions to help people on low incomes to afford to buy certain things that are becoming more expensive could also play a significant role. In addition, it will be important to consider these price trends when making adjustments in benefits, tax credits, the minimum wage and public sector pay, in order to take more account of how the real minimum cost of living is rising.

Global connections and UK communities – challenges and opportunities

Migration and new communications technology have contributed to the extensive links between people in the UK and other parts of the world. Local and devolved governments are exploring how to maximise their global links for the benefit of their areas. It is important to carry out further analysis of the different approaches and impacts of these strategies to attract investments and to build social inclusion, and to consider how these could maximise benefits for disadvantaged people and places locally.

New communications technology enables global links, but it is not accessible or taken up by everyone – people on low incomes are significantly over-represented in the group without Internet connectivity. The research shows that it is important that the Digital Inclusion Strategy maintains a focus on complementary skills, confidence and attitudes as well as access to technology, to ensure that people are equally able to take up the opportunities that new technology and global links can offer. Future projects could also usefully consider how civil society groups can make the most of linking with partners in other parts of the world, both to facilitate mutual learning and to develop analysis and action on shared global concerns relevant to poverty eradication.

Global links can raise complex challenges for local areas, particularly with the movements of people and rapid flows of information between local areas. The research has identified examples of good practice in local areas in responding to these challenges, which include the establishment of communities of practice and also distribution of information to frontline workers about external events of relevance. It is important to ensure that this sharing of good practice within and between local areas continues, and that this is complemented by signposting to useful resources at the national level.

UK policy-making in a global policy arena: implications for addressing poverty and inequality

Global governance covers a range of issues relevant to poverty and inequality in the UK. However, there is limited awareness of how it works, where decisions are made and how to influence them. Research suggests that there is more that civil society organisations and others could do both to build public understanding of global governance mechanisms and to use the opportunities these provide through their monitoring, peer pressure and learning functions to benefit UK communities and help to tackle poverty.

The JRF 'Globalisation, UK poverty and communities' programme suggests that the costs and benefits of globalisation are unevenly distributed, with people's experiences being influenced by their own and their local areas' history and existing resources and capacities. It raises the question: how can global processes be shaped in the UK, to avoid exacerbating existing inequalities, and to decrease regional and other differences in employment and wider social outcomes? This is particularly pertinent at a time when the Government is declaring its intention to increasingly devolve power to local areas. Further multi-disciplinary exploration of the potential and the limits of different players at the local, regional and national levels would help to inform future national and local policy in the UK, with the aim of contributing to poverty eradication and the creation of vibrant communities in the future.

⇨ From *Globalisation, UK poverty and communities* by Teresa Hanley, published in 2011 by the Joseph Rowntree Foundation. Reproduced by permission of the JRF.

© Joseph Rowntree Foundation

Trade footprint

'I'd like to tell people the coffee they're enjoying now is the cause of all our problems. We grow it with our sweat and sell it for nothing.' Lawrence Seguya, a coffee farmer

Trade is the buying and selling of goods and services

Trade between various countries of the world has taken place for thousands of years and has enabled people to obtain food, resources and materials that they could not produce for themselves.

So what is your trade footprint?

Put simply, this is the amount of goods and services you use and consume that have been traded (bought and transported from other countries). The size of your trade footprint is affected by the amount of land, resources, water and energy involved in manufacturing or transporting traded items.

How far does your trade footprint reach today?

Try to measure your trade footprint! Look at the clothes you wear, the toys and games you play with, the food and drink you consume in one day: Where do they come from? How far have they travelled? How did they travel to you? What resources were used to make them and transport them to you? You may be surprised to see just how connected you are to the world through trade! And just how BIG your trade footprint is!

The trade footprint: how it measures up

⇨ International trade is worth $10 million a minute. But poor countries only receive $40,000, or 0.4%, of this trade.

⇨ Rich countries spend $320 billion each year on subsidising agriculture – six times the amount they spend on foreign aid.

⇨ The average European cow is subsidised by around $800. Ethiopia's total national income per person, per year is around $100.

⇨ If a jar of coffee purchased in a supermarket costs £3, just 3p (1%) goes to the coffee grower.

⇨ If Africa, East Asia, South Asia and Latin America were each to increase their share of world exports by just one per cent, the resulting increase in income could lift 128 million people out of poverty.

⇨ Information from HEC Global Learning Centre and the Global Footprints website: www.globalfootprints.org

© HEC Global Learning Centre/Global Footprints

The problem with bananas

Information from BananaLink.

Most bananas are grown for export on large plantations in Latin America and, increasingly, Africa. The monoculture production methods used can destroy entire ecosystems. The banana industry consumes more agrochemicals than any other in the world, excepting cotton. Some of these chemicals are classified as hazardous by the World Health Organization. Agrochemical use pollutes water supplies and can have devastating impacts on worker health. Small-scale production in these regions and the Caribbean is more sustainable but low prices have forced many farmers out of the international market.

Corporate power

Just a handful of multinational fruit companies control 75% of the international banana trade – Dole, Del Monte, Chiquita, Fyffes and Noboa – but supermarkets are now the most powerful actors along the banana supply chain and make substantial profits by paying unsustainably low prices to the fruit companies that market bananas and/or own plantations.

The 'race to the bottom'

A 'race to the bottom' in the banana industry has been fuelled by the low prices paid by supermarkets and the cost-cutting actions taken by fruit companies as they relocate in search of cheaper labour and weaker legislation in exporting regions. Employers have increasingly sub-contracted labour in a bid to reduce their responsibility for working conditions, the respect of core labour standards or payment of a living wage. Plantation labour is increasingly casual, with many workers on temporary contracts or hired on a daily basis. In several countries, membership of independent trade unions has fallen as a direct result.

Plantation conditions are harsh, with workers toiling ten to 12 hours in unbearable heat up to six days a week. Many workers fail to earn a 'living wage' to cover their basic needs such as housing, food, clothing and education.

Who earns what from field to supermarket?

The diagram opposite (based on a typical Latin American banana sold in the UK in 2010) illustrates how unfairly value from the sale of bananas is distributed along the supply chain. Retailers can take up to 45% of monies compared to the plantation and packhouse workers who take as little as 2.5%.

Supermarket price wars

Bananas are the single biggest profit-making item sold on UK supermarket shelves. They are frequently a weapon of choice in the price wars pursued by our major supermarkets. Over the last few years banana prices have been pushed down to ridiculously low levels, sometimes to as little as 36 pence per kilo – or two-thirds less than they were in 2002!

Just a handful of multinational fruit companies control 75% of the international banana trade

Although supermarkets sometimes fund these price wars, in general the cuts are simply passed onto suppliers until they reach plantation workers, the weakest link in the chain and therefore the 'easiest' to squeeze. Workers are, however, the ones that can least afford the cuts. Their tiny share of total value often fails to provide a living wage (to cover essential needs including food, housing and education). The majority of plantation workers live in poverty and too many still have their most basic labour rights abused.

⇨ The above information is reprinted with kind permission from BananaLink. Visit http://bananalink. org.uk for more information.

© BananaLink

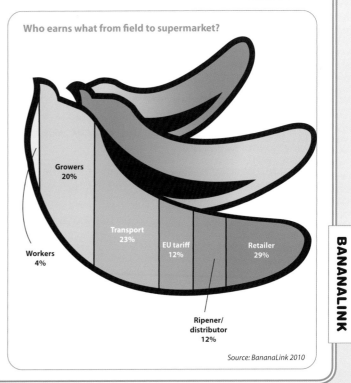

Who earns what from field to supermarket?

Growers 20%

Transport 23%

Workers 4%

EU tariff 12%

Retailer 29%

Ripener/ distributor 12%

Source: BananaLink 2010

BANANALINK

What is Fairtrade?

Not all trade is fair! Farmers and workers at the beginning of the chain don't always get a fair share of the benefits of trade. Fairtrade enables consumers to put this right.

Introducing Fairtrade

Fairtrade is an alternative approach to conventional trade and is based on a partnership between producers and consumers. Fairtrade offers producers a better deal and improved terms of trade. This allows them the opportunity to improve their lives and plan for their future. Fairtrade offers consumers a powerful way to reduce poverty through their everyday shopping.

When a product carries the FAIRTRADE Mark it means the producers and traders have met Fairtrade Standards. The Standards are designed to address the imbalance of power in trading relationships, unstable markets and the injustices of conventional trade.

The Charter of Fair Trade Principles

In 2009, Fairtrade International (FLO) along with the World Fair Trade Organization adopted the Charter of Fair Trade Principles, which provides a single international reference point for Fair Trade. The charter includes our common vision, definition of Fair Trade, core principles and the distinct approaches to Fair Trade. FLO endorses the definition of Fair Trade and adheres to the principles.

The Standards

There are two distinct sets of Fairtrade Standards, which acknowledge different types of disadvantaged producers. One set of standards applies to smallholders that are working together in co-operatives or other organisations with a democratic structure. The other set applies to workers, whose employers pay decent wages, guarantee the right to join trade unions, ensure health and safety standards and provide adequate housing where relevant.

Fairtrade Standards also cover terms of trade. Most products have a Fairtrade Price, which is the minimum that must be paid to the producers. In addition, producers get an additional sum, the Fairtrade Premium, to invest in their communities.

Fairtrade prices

The minimum price paid to Fairtrade producers is determined by the Fairtrade Standards. It applies to most Fairtrade certified products. This price aims to ensure that producers can cover their average costs of sustainable production. It acts as a safety net for farmers at times when world markets fall below a sustainable level. Without this, farmers are completely at the mercy of the market.

When the market price is higher than the Fairtrade minimum, the buyer must pay the higher price. Producers and traders can also negotiate higher prices on the basis of quality and other attributes.

The Fairtrade Premium

In addition to the Fairtrade price, there is an additional sum of money, called the Fairtrade Premium. This money goes into a communal fund for workers and farmers to use to improve their social, economic and environmental conditions.

The use of this additional income is decided upon democratically by producers within the farmers' organisation, or by workers on a plantation. The Premium is invested in education and healthcare, farm improvements to increase yield and quality, or processing facilities to increase income.

As many projects funded by the Premium are communal, the broader community outside the producer organisation often benefits from Fairtrade.

Fairtrade products

There are now thousands of products that carry the FAIRTRADE Mark. Fairtrade standards exist for food products ranging from tea and coffee to fresh fruits and nuts. There are also standards for non-food products such as flowers and plants, sports balls and seed cotton.

Who is behind Fairtrade?

The following organisations are behind Fairtrade:

Fairtrade International (FLO)

FLO is a non-profit, multi-stakeholder body that is responsible for the strategic direction of Fairtrade, sets Fairtrade standards and supports producers.

FLO-CERT

FLO-CERT is an independent certification company, owned by FLO. FLO-CERT inspects producers and traders to ensure they comply with Fairtrade standards.

Fairtrade standards exist for food products ranging from tea and coffee to fresh fruits and nuts. There are also standards for non-food products such as flowers and plants, sports balls and seed cotton

Fairtrade labelling initiatives

These are national organisations that market Fairtrade in their country. There are currently 19 Fairtrade labelling initiatives covering 23 countries in Europe, North America, Japan, Australia and New Zealand. These organisations also licence companies to use the FAIRTRADE Mark on products in their country.

Fairtrade producer networks

These are associations that Fairtrade-certified producer groups may join. There are currently three producer networks, representing producers in Africa, Asia and Latin America and the Caribbean. Through these networks, Fairtrade producers can influence decisions that affect their future.

Fairtrade marketing organisations

These are national organisations that market and promote Fairtrade in their country, similar to labelling initiatives. Fairtrade International directly licenses companies in these countries to use the FAIRTRADE Certification Mark. There are currently two Fairtrade marketing organisations, in South Africa and in the Czech Republic.

⇨ The above information is reprinted with kind permission from Fairtrade International. Visit www.fairtrade.net for more information.

© Fairtrade International

Fairtrade facts and figures

Fairtrade has experienced impressive growth. In the last four years global sales have more than tripled and hundreds more producer organisations have become certified.

A success story

More than 1.2 million producers and workers in 58 developing countries now benefit from global Fairtrade sales.

Over the last 20 years, sales of Fairtrade-certified products have increased phenomenally. Marginalised farming communities throughout the developing world now benefit from fairer terms of trade.

In 2009, Fairtrade-certified sales amounted to approximately €3.4 billion worldwide

Through growing consumer support, Fairtrade has now achieved significant market share in many product categories in the 70 countries where Fairtrade products are sold. In some national markets, Fairtrade accounts for between 20–50% of market share in certain products.

Growing number of producer organisations

There are now 827 Fairtrade-certified producer organisations in 58 producing countries, representing over 1.2 million farmers and workers. In addition to other benefits, approximately €52 million was distributed to communities in 2009 for use in community development. Including families and dependents, Fairtrade International estimates that six million people directly benefit from Fairtrade.

Sales of Fairtrade products

The sales of Fairtrade-certified products grew 15% between 2008–2009. In 2009, Fairtrade-certified sales amounted to approximately €3.4 billion worldwide.

⇨ Information from Fairtrade International. Visit www.fairtrade.net for more information.

© Fairtrade International

FAIRTRADE INTERNATIONAL

Ethical shopping

Information from YouGov.

Many UK consumers would prefer to shop at stores with reputable ethics records that exhibit corporate social responsibility, but a much smaller number buy exclusively from companies whose ethics they agree with, says a recent report by YouGov SixthSense into the ethical shopping practices of UK consumers.

Corporate Social Responsibility (CSR) is a concept that seeks to bring business and manufacturing practices into line with widely accepted ethical standards so that companies' business practices are compatible with the rights and wellbeing of all members of the public sphere.

While seven out of ten shoppers say they like shopping with companies who 'visibly give something back to society'... only 30% say they manage to buy solely from companies that conform to their ethical standards

Half of UK consumers say that they would like to buy from companies that have a strong CSR programme in place, yet, in a blow to rights watchdogs and charities that seek to ensure CSR is widely implemented, 61% of consumers say they hear a lot about the concept but 'nothing of any substance'.

Similarly, while seven out of ten shoppers say they like shopping with companies who 'visibly give something back to society' and 81% of UK consumers say that they do not like buying products from companies they 'disapprove of', only 30% say they manage to buy solely from companies that conform to their ethical standards.

Many UK consumers would prefer to shop at stores with reputable ethics records that exhibit corporate social responsibility

Commenting on the report findings, James McCoy, Research Director for YouGov SixthSense, explains that cost can be the stumbling block over which companies fall in delivering what could satisfy a seemingly popular consumer demand. 'Openly submitting to CSR norms can only help a company's reputation, but that high esteem does not transpose easily into financial rewards or a loyal consumer base, especially in a recessionary period.' He continued, 'Awareness and consumption of Fairtrade products is high but only because Fairtrade practices have become *modus operandi* without unduly raising the cost of the product.'

11 September 2010

⇨ The above information is reprinted with kind permission from YouGov. Visit www.yougov.com for more information.

© YouGov

OF COURSE WE'D PREFER TO BUY FROM SHOPS WITH A HIGH ETHICAL STANDARD BUT...

Freeing the ultimate resource

Information from the Adam Smith Institute.

By Sam Bowman

What's the single best policy change that could be made to reduce poverty and boost global GDP growth? Many would say the elimination of trade barriers. Unfortunately, many would probably suggest a 'big push' of development aid money. But a new paper in the *Journal of Economic Perspectives* argues that the most positive change that could be made by far is the elimination of barriers to migration.

The paper, which is free to download, compares the existing academic estimates for global GDP efficiency increases from the elimination of trade barriers with those from eliminating migration barriers. Free trade estimates are around 1–5%, or between $600 billion and $3 trillion. This is a substantial figure and would be a huge boost to people in poor countries, since most of it would probably accrue there. But the jaw-dropping estimates for open borders make the boost from free trade benefits look like pocket money.

The existing academic literature suggests that eliminating legal restrictions on migration could increase global GDP by between 67% and 147%. Global GDP is about $58 trillion, so that means the bottom end of the scale would be around $39 trillion. That's an astonishing figure, and would change the world if it was achieved.

The paper discusses the reasons for these huge figures, including the question that I think is most important – is labour productivity mostly about who you are, or where you are? If it's the latter, then it's not hard to see why things would improve so much if more labour was located in the West. As Adam Smith said, all you really need for prosperity is peace, easy taxes and a tolerable administration of justice. Compared with the world's poor countries, we in the West have these things in abundance.

Naturally, this money doesn't just fall from the sky – the high estimates are contingent on a very high amount of emigration from poor countries to rich ones. Would so many people be prepared to move? And how much of the money would flow back to the home countries through remittances, where it would be most useful? Both are unclear and difficult to predict, as the paper admits. And I'm always sceptical of economic predictions that claim much precision. But, really, these are all beside the point. However imprecise the estimate and predictions, the evidence is quite consistent that opening barriers to migration would deliver enormous boosts to global GDP that are far beyond most of the other policy options currently on the menu.

When I write posts in support of more migration, I either get replies that (a) the welfare state couldn't take it, or (b) we need to protect our culture. I have some sympathy for both arguments. My response to (a) is fairly simple – most people in poor countries who want to move to rich ones do so because they want to work and earn money for their families, not because they want to be parasites. The welfare state perverts incentives to work, but it does so for native populations as well as immigrants – indeed, the evidence in the UK suggests that it's immigrants who are willing to take low-paid jobs and Britons who stay at home collecting benefit cheques. There's a significant problem here, but it's far from being an immigrant-only one.

If a 'welfare-lite' package for immigrants – say, provision of non-rivalrous services like roads and streetlights that would be impractical to withhold, and a rolling-out of the full array of the welfare state after a certain number of months or years in employment – would make immigration more politically feasible, fine. I doubt it would put many would-be immigrants off.

Argument (b) strikes me as a fundamentally anti-property stance to take, though I understand the thinking behind it. Yes, national culture is extremely valuable, but not at the expense of people's private property rights. If a homeowner wants to rent out her spare room, what right does the state have to tell her whom she may and may not rent it out to? If an employer wants to hire someone, I do not want the state to be able to dictate what nationalities they can choose from. Immigrant ghettoisation is a big problem, but mostly a state-made one.

Some arguments against immigration have merit and shouldn't be dismissed. But the evidence of the enormous gains to wealth that open borders would bring should diminish their weight. If opening borders could deliver even a fraction of the huge gains suggested by the academic literature, it should be the priority for people interested in fighting poverty.

As Julian Simon said, people are the 'ultimate resource'. Allowing that ultimate resource to move across borders freely would be a massive step towards a freer, richer world.

22 August 2011

⇨ The above information is reprinted with kind permission from the Adam Smith Institute. Visit www. adamsmith.org for more information.

ADAM SMITH INSTITUTE

KEY FACTS

⇨ Ways need to be found to manage and structure globalisation so that it supports fundamental human rights and sustainable development, and generates prosperity for ordinary people, particularly the poorest. (page 2)

⇨ Europe's need for resources could in coming decades be matched by those of China, India, Brazil and others, putting even greater pressure on the environment. (page 3)

⇨ In 2004 the World Bank provided $20.1 billion for 245 projects in developing countries worldwide, with its finance and/or technical expertise aimed at helping those countries reduce poverty. (page 9)

⇨ Under the enhanced Heavily Indebted Poor Countries (HIPC) Initiative, 26 poor countries have received debt relief which will save them $41 billion over time. (page 10)

⇨ The IMF was founded more than 60 years ago toward the end of World War II. The founders aimed to build a framework for economic cooperation that would avoid a repetition of the disastrous economic policies that had contributed to the Great Depression of the 1930s and the global conflict that followed. (page 11)

⇨ There is no doubt globalisation has brought many benefits: exotic holidays, solidarity and information sharing, to name a few. However, it is important to remember there are negative aspects too: for example, indigenous customs and languages are disappearing and small local businesses and farms are being swallowed up by large multinationals. (page 13)

⇨ Multinational corporations control over 33% of the world's productive assets and over 70% of world trade, but only account for 5% of the world's employment. (page 13)

⇨ The incidence of hunger is more widespread than ever before in human history, surpassing one billion people in 2009 despite the record harvests of food being reaped in recent years. (page 17)

⇨ At least 1.4 billion people live in extreme poverty, a number equivalent to more than four times the population of the United States. (page 17)

⇨ Britain has become a hub in the global web of car and engine production. This year, 1.4 million cars and more than three million engines will be produced here, most of them for export. (page 22)

⇨ In Britain, the Institute for Fiscal Studies says that our real disposable incomes are in the midst of a 14-year freeze. (page 24)

⇨ In 2008 Fairtrade chocolate made up less than one per cent of the market in the UK. By the end of 2010, it made up around ten per cent and reached the milestone of £1 billion in sales. (page 26)

⇨ World trade is dominated by 80,000 multinational corporations (MNCs), large companies with a presence in many parts of the world. MNCs account for 70 per cent of world trade. (page 27)

⇨ Trade has a direct impact on poverty: on average, an increase in trade volumes of 10% will raise incomes by 5%. (page 28)

⇨ The 48 poorest countries, home to ten per cent of the world's population, have seen their share of exports decline to less than half a per cent of the world total in the last 20 years. (page 32)

⇨ International trade is worth $10 million a minute. But poor countries only receive $40,000 or 0.4% of this trade. (page 34)

⇨ Just a handful of multinational fruit companies control 75% of the international banana trade. (page 35)

⇨ The sales of Fairtrade-certified products grew 15% between 2008–2009. In 2009, Fairtrade certified sales amounted to approximately €3.4 billion worldwide. (page 37)

Fair trade

A movement which advocates fair prices, improved working conditions and better trade terms for producers in developing countries. Exports from developing countries that have been certified Fairtrade – which include products such as coffee, tea, honey, cocoa, chocolate, sugar, cotton and bananas – carry the Fairtrade mark.

Free trade

An economic policy which promotes the free movement of goods and services between countries and the elimination of restrictions to trading between nations, such as import and export tariffs.

Gross Domestic Product (GDP)

The value of all the goods and services produced in a country within a year.

Globalisation

Globalisation is a term used to explain the increased social and trade-related exchanges between nations. It implies that nations are moving closer together economically and culturally. In recent years, through the Internet, air travel, trade and popular culture, globalisation has rapidly increased.

International Monetary Fund (IMF)

The International Monetary Fund (IMF) is an international organisation set up to oversee the global financial system and stabilise exchange rates.

Liberalisation

The relaxation of government restrictions such as barriers to free trade.

Multinational corporations (MNCs)

Powerful companies which operate in more than one country. Due to their size and large economies, multinational corporations – sometimes called transnational corporations (TNCs) – can hold substantial influence over governments and local economies.

NAMA

The World Trade Organization members negotiate on many different areas in order to increase liberalisation.

Agriculture and public services (GATS) are two of the more well known areas. Another is called non-agricultural market access (NAMA). These negotiations aim to remove barriers to free trade in all industrial goods and natural resources. For example, NAMA seeks to take down import tariffs, which make imported goods more expensive.

Protectionism

The policy of protecting domestic industries from foreign competition by restricting trade between nations.

Sovereign debt

In the 1970s, rich oil-producing countries put their massive profits into banks to earn interest. To pay this interest, the banks made loans to developing countries. Interest rates were low, and these loans were thought to be affordable. It hardly mattered what the loans were used for because the borrowing governments guaranteed the debt. This is called 'sovereign debt'.

Tariffs

A tax placed on imported and exported goods.

Trade

When you buy a computer game or a bar of chocolate, you are 'trading': exchanging money for goods. Workers, companies, countries and consumers take part in trade. Workers make or grow the goods. Companies pay the workers and sell what they produce. Governments encourage companies to set up; they create jobs, generate taxes and earn foreign currency. Consumers buy the end product.

World Bank

An organisation set up to reduce poverty by providing loans for developing countries.

World Trade Organization (WTO)

An international organisation first set up in 1995 to monitor the rules of international trade and promote free trade between countries. The WTO has the power to impose fines or sanctions on member countries that do not follow the rules of trade. Critics of the WTO argue that it holds too much power and protects the interests of rich countries to the disadvantage of developing countries.

ACKNOWLEDGEMENTS

The publisher is grateful for permission to reproduce the following material.

While every care has been taken to trace and acknowledge copyright, the publisher tenders its apology for any accidental infringement or where copyright has proved untraceable. The publisher would be pleased to come to a suitable arrangement in any such case with the rightful owner.

Chapter One: Globalisation

Globalisation: key issues, © Trades Union Congress (TUC), Living in an interconnected world, © European Environment Agency, Debt, © CAFOD, Understanding the World Trade Organization, © World Trade Organization, What is the World Bank?, © World Bank, The International Monetary Fund (IMF), © International Monetary Fund, Globalisation and identity, © World Trade Organization, Frequently asked questions on globalisation, free trade, the WTO and NAMA, © Friends of the Earth, 2012 could see Globalisation 2.0 take off, © Guardian News & Media Ltd 2012, Rethinking the global economy: the case for sharing, © Share the World's Resources, Globalisation and the rise of the global middle class, © Center for American Progress, Globalisation can work, but only with a unified international plan, © Guardian News & Media Ltd 2012, Globalisation has turned on its Western creators, © Telegraph Media Group Limited 2011.

Chapter Two: Global Trade

Trade, © CAFOD, Trade and economic growth, © Crown copyright is reproduced with the permission of Her Majesty's Stationery Office, Questions and answers on trade, © ActionAid, Trade glossary, © HEC Global Learning Centre/Global Footprints website, Markets, poverty and Fair Trade, © Adam Smith Institute, Put your best foot forward: the theory of free trade, © HEC Global Learning Centre/Global Footprints website, Globalisation, UK poverty and communities, © Joseph Rowntree Foundation, Trade footprint, © HEC Global Learning Centre/Global Footprints website, The problem with bananas, © BananaLink, What is Fairtrade?, © Fairtrade International, Fairtrade facts and figures, © Fairtrade International, Ethical shopping, © YouGov, Freeing the ultimate resource, © Adam Smith Institute.

Illustrations

Pages 2, 15, 22: Angelo Madrid; pages 7, 17, 24, 38: Don Hatcher; pages 9, 36: Bev Aisbett; pages 11, 20, 25: Simon Kneebone.

Cover photography

Left: © Svilen Milev (www.efffective.com). Centre: © Jakub Krechowicz. Right: © Sanja Gjenero.

Additional acknowledgements

Research by Carolyn Kirby on behalf of Independence Educational Publishers.

With thanks to the Independence team: Cara Acred, Mary Chapman, Sandra Dennis and Jan Sunderland.

Lisa Firth
Cambridge
April, 2012

The following tasks aim to help you think through the debates surrounding globalisation and provide a better understanding of the topic.

1 Is globalisation a threat to identity? Discuss your views in small groups.

2 Save the packaging from everything which makes up your evening meal one night in the week (make sure the packaging shows the food's country of origin: if this is not given, see if you can find this information on the manufacturer's website). Take the packaging with you to class and, in groups of five, make a list of all the countries which have contributed to your evening meals. How many food miles have your meals travelled?

3 The World Bank, IMF and World Trade Organization are sometimes called the 'Bretton Woods institutions'. What is the historical reason for this? Research the formation and history of these organisations and present your findings in the form of a timeline.

4 Plan an event which could be used to promote fair trade products during Fair Trade Fortnight.

5 Find out about the Tescopoly campaign. What are the campaign's grievances, and what actions have they taken to address these? Write a summary of the campaign, stating whether or not you agree with its stated aims.

6 'Globalisation has its detractors, but it is primarily a force for good, triggering an overall increase in living standards and wealth generation.' Do you agree with this opinion? Debate this statement in groups, with half of you arguing in favour and the other half against.

7 Imagine you are the CEO of a major multinational corporation. List the ten rules of corporate social responsibility that you would wish your company to be guided by in order to prevent globalisation causing damage to those in the developing world.

8 Create a Monopoly-like board game to help people understand the problems of globalisation.

9 Read *Globalisation and identity* on page 12. Do you agree with Pascal Lamy's assessment of globalisation? Write a response, stating why you support or oppose Mr Lamy's position.

10 What impact has globalisation had on the environment? Does the world need to focus on a more sustainable trade model in the future? Write an analysis of this issue.

11 'Why should I worry about the impact of my company's actions on the developing world? My responsibility is to my shareholders, who expect me to maximise profits. Let governments worry about regulating trade.' Write a response to this company CEO, explaining why they should be concerned about trading responsibly.

12 How has the rise of communications technology such as the Internet and mobile phones affected globalisation? Plan and write an article examining this phenomenon.

13 Design and conduct a survey among people in your year group to find out how many of them live in a household which purchases fair trade goods. Present your findings as a set of graphs.

14 Write a diary entry covering a day in the life of a developing-world farmer struggling to compete with the large multinationals also operating in his region.

15 Imagine you are setting up a new campaign group which would encourage people to buy ethically-produced food and clothing. Design a name, logo and slogan for your campaign.

16 'This house believes that free trade is the best way out of poverty for developing countries.' Debate this motion as a class, with one half arguing in favour and the other against.

17 Imagine you are an MP voting in parliament on whether developing countries should have their debts cancelled in order to boost their economies. How would you decide to vote? Explain your answer.